The Start-up Business Guide

50 First Steps:
The Critical Tasks Every Successful Founder Completes in their 1st Year

By Shan Naqvi & Jacob Aldridge

Website:
https://www.thestartupbusinessguide.com

Copyright © 2020 Shan Naqvi & Jacob Aldridge

All rights reserved. No part of this book may be reproduced in any form or by any electronic or mechanical means, including information storage and retrieval systems, without permission in writing from the publisher, except by reviewers, who may quote brief passages in a review.

ISBNs
Paperback: 978-0-6487622-0-1
eBook: 978-0-6487622-1-8

 A catalogue record for this work is available from the National Library of Australia

Cover Design by
Ubaid Qabool ubaidqabool@gmail.com

Contact Shan Naqvi shan@sahnnaqvi.com
Contact Jacob Aldridge jacob@jacobaldridge.com
Visit www.thestartupbusinessguide.com

Shan Naqvi

To my dad, Ghulam Murtaza Shah, my mother and my family. Thank you for the support that guided me to do this. There are not enough words in the universe to express the depth of the love and appreciation I have for you.

Jacob Aldridge

To Mrs Pat Godfrey. You taught me Literature, in written word and silver screen. Consider this a promise kept.

Prologue

Jacob Aldridge

Starting a business has never been easier. Surviving in business continues to be as challenging as ever.

For all the raw emotion of being a start-up business owner, the highest highs and lowest lows, it remains the case that half of all new businesses have closed within three years.

We want to change that.

My belief, in the information age, is that there's often too many opinions and too much data for small business owners to work from. While this may not be the only book you'll ever read about your business, we have aimed to be practical and comprehensive enough that you come here first before becoming lost on Google.

Shan Naqvi

I've written this book to help people. When I started my career as an entrepreneur, nobody was there to support me and I became lost in the confusing variety of guidance online.

There was a moment when I was very close to giving up, but I didn't. Lucky, that. I didn't quit where so many others do.

Business really taught me what life really is. You have to take on all your responsibilities in business. Sometimes you're going to suffer, too. But it's going to teach you lessons. That could change your whole life and make you stronger and stronger.

So here you're neither lucky nor anything but, initially, business is your own hard work. This tells you that whatever you are now, it's just because of you. And that's the inspiration. *The Great Inspiration.*

That's why I choose business because of a job. And I want to help people make a decision in their lives to be successful entrepreneurs. And make a beautiful life.

One thing I really learned from interviewing so many of the businessmen is that they were all struggling in their early days. At some point, they all lost. It doesn't matter how big they are today. But they're very close to everyone they've had to go through difficulties.

But they've changed their lives. Not only do they change their lives, but they have changed the lives of their entire family.

This book is a compilation of the things I wish someone could have told me when I started.

I am sharing them with you, to help you make a better life.

How to read this book

You're not supposed to read this whole book before you take action. There is order to the first 20 Chapters; after that, the Steps may be done in different orders and every business owner's needs will vary.

Familiarise yourself with the Contents page: if a heading feels relevant (like Pricing or Cash Flow) then skip ahead.

And don't leave this on a shelf once read! Whether it's returning to the dog-eared paperback on your desk or printing key chapters to share with your team, we know that you will return to this advice year after year.

These 50 Steps (plus your bonus features) aren't all necessary, though together they are likely sufficient to guarantee your business success.

And they're not exclusive to your first year – this is a guide you can lean on as you successfully grow your business in the second year, the third year, and we hope into the decades ahead.

About Jacob Aldridge

By Shan Naqvi

Jacob Aldridge is an eye-catching and very handsome business consultant, partner, presenter and keynote speaker based in Australia. Beauty is nothing without brain, as they say. He's blessed with both beauty and brain. Jacob lives the life most people have dreamed of living, and since his early days, he's a canny person. His vision was clear as to where to put efforts to improve business outcomes. As a budding perpetual traveller, Jacob and his beautiful wife continue to work and travel around the world even since the arrival of their baby daughter in 2019. Many of the Chapters written in this book in the first person are from Jacob's specific experience in one of his own businesses, or among the many hundred he has coached around the world. Jacob is a Guinness world record holder, a published author, and a TV host. He, as an international business coach, partner and consultant, has worked with more than 300 privately owned companies in a wide range of industries around the world. Most of his personal clients are energetic young businesses, mainly professional service firms with between 12 and 96 employees per venue. His career has seen him work with growing companies around Australia and around the world, both in person and using technology to provide constant support and guidance given the nomadic lifestyle he leads.

Alumni clients and colleagues describe Jacob as a smart and creative entrepreneur who makes things happen, bringing the special energy that comes from the conviction that business is best when it's enjoyable.

As a Keynote Speaker and MC, Jacob's experience includes: Dent's *Key Person of Influence*; the *Family Law Practitioners Association* Conference; *Happy Lawyer Happy Life* Retreat; *Annual Leadership of Principals and Property Professionals Summit*; *Generation YOU*; *World Business and Executive Coach Summit (WBECS)*; and the *Email Marketing Summit Australia (EMSA)*.

About Shan Naqvi

By Jacob Aldridge

About once a week for the past ten years, I receive an approach from an aspiring business owner. Most "don't know what they don't know", and are just seeking some reassurance that they have what it takes to start and successfully grow a business. Sadly, many of these individuals never make the leap into entrepreneurship. I know this, because my standard advice is to do some market research and come back to me with what they learn: for the 40 or so people who speak with me per year, less than five have the next conversation. Fewer of them respond with the speed and drive necessary for business success. **Shan Naqvi is one of those few.** Shan approached me about a year ago, immediately distinctive because he wanted to give me something as well as ask me questions. I was one of many interviews Shan completed with business coaches, leaders, and founders around the world – some of which form the backbone of this guide. As the idea of this Start-up Business Guide began to form, Shan demonstrated to me the two fundamental characteristics I look for in a business partner. He was vulnerable enough to ask for help with his challenges (we all have them); and he was reliable enough to follow through on every commitment, always in a timely manner. Shan lives in Pakistan close to his wider family, and coincidentally barely an hour's drive from where my own grandmother was born. Yet his (like mine) is a truly global vision, to impact business owners regardless of borders. It has been my honour and pleasure to work beside Shan in creating this Guide, and to be part of him achieving his ambitions to help so many others.

Jacob Eldridge

About Your Free Bonus Features

Thank you for investing in The Start-up Business Guide. Your return on investment doesn't end here!

Visit **www.thestartupbusinessguide.com** to access this whole collection of bonus features valued at over $1,997:

- 10 BONUS Chapters
- All 134 Episodes of our Business Owner Video Series
- Two free business books: *More Money, More Time, Less Stress* and *Thrive, not Survive*
- The Brandonian Brand Archetype Indicator
- Free Quote for Building Your Website
- The Contextual Business Plan Template
- The Start-up Business Cash Flow Forecast Template
- Daily 2 Month Projection Cash Flow Forecast
- *What is Business Strategy* Whitepaper
- Skills Matrix Template for your Training Analysis
- Our Recommended Reading List
  And much more...

When you sign up as a Member, use the code STARTMEUP to access these features exclusively available to those who have purchased this book.

TABLE OF CONTENTS

Like Swimming (and Sex) 1
    Chapter 1 1
Mindset 5
    Chapter 2 5
Emotions of a Start-up 10
    Chapter 3 10
Don't Copy the Wrong Homework 15
    Chapter 4 15
Top 3 Priorities 20
    Chapter 5 20
Target Market 25
    Chapter 6 25
Value Proposition 28
    Chapter 7 28
Validating Ideas 32
    Chapter 8 32
Structures 38
    Chapter 9 38
Brand and Name 42
    Chapter 10 42
Start-up Digital Footprint 52
    Chapter 11 52
Product 59
    Chapter 12 59

Pricing 62
    Chapter 13 62
Business Model 66
    Chapter 14 66
Break Even Formula 73
    Chapter 15 73
RNR Colors: Roles 'n' Responsibilities for Rest 'n' Recuperation 80
    Chapter 16 80
Work Flows 85
    Chapter 17 85
Key Relationships 1 of 3- Accountant 91
    Chapter 18 91
Key Relationship 2 of 3- Mentor 95
    Chapter 19 95
Context vs Content 99
    Chapter 20 99
Layers of Context 104
    Chapter 21 104
Commercial Vision 111
    Chapter 22 111
Cultural Vision 116
    Chapter 23 116
Risk Profile 120
    Chapter 24 120
4 Critical Partnership Questions - Strategic 124
    Chapter 25 124
4 Critical Partnership Questions - Operational 133

Chapter 26 133
Key Financial Metrics 139
Chapter 27 139
Personal vs Business Finances 143
Chapter 28 143
Making Investment Decisions 148
Chapter 29 148
Cash Flow 157
Chapter 30 157
Debtors (and Creditors) 169
Chapter 31 169
Ask: Do I Need Funding? 175
Chapter 32 175
Pivots 182
Chapter 33 182
Team 186
Chapter 34 186
Hiring Your First Team Member 193
Chapter 35 193
Growth / Capacity 201
Chapter 36 201
Customers: Advocates or Assassins 208
Chapter 37 208
Marketing Structure 213
Chapter 38 213
Bullseye Framework 218

Chapter 39 218
Sales Hourglass 224
Chapter 40 224
Sales Meeting 230
Chapter 41 230
Critical Numbers: Sales 237
Chapter 41 237
Referrals from Client Program 242
Chapter 43 242
Client Service Program 249
Chapter 44 249
Testimonials / Case Studies 253
Chapter 45 253
Skill Development 258
Chapter 46 258
Premises 265
Chapter 47 265
Leveraging Technology 271
Chapter 48 271
Suppliers 275
Chapter 49 275
One More Piece of Information 280
Chapter 50 280

Like Swimming (and Sex)

Chapter 1

Our belief is that entrepreneurship – starting your own business – has things in common with swimming and with sex: You can't learn how to do any of them from reading a book. At some point, you just have to jump in, see what it feels like, and practice until you improve.

So why did we write a book about something you can't learn from a book! Because, like with swimming and sex, we want you to be safe when you plunge into the exhilarating world of owning your own business.

You are about to embark (or maybe you already have) on a grand journey, perhaps the most exciting and rewarding of your life. It is only once you are on that journey that you can truly understand what entrepreneurship is all about – the great times, and the terrible burdens. No book you ever read can replace that first-hand experience.

As adults, we learn from experience. Our belief for start-up business owners is this: you can either learn from your own experience, slowly and expensively; or you can learn from the experience of others, avoiding the common errors and accelerating towards your outcomes. This guide is designed to bring that experience from others.

What you will learn through all 50 Steps we discuss comes from our own experience as business owners, and more valuably from interviews with and insight from more than 1,000 other small business owners who were once in your shoes.

Sometimes we quote them directly; other times we are more direct with our guidance, or explanation of key concepts or tools that you can use in your business.

We can't guarantee you success in your venture, but we will improve your odds of success. We believe that the only way to truly fail in business is not to take risks, not to jump in to the pool and start swimming.

Because even if your first business, this beautiful baby you are thinking of bringing into the world, doesn't succeed – that doesn't make *you* a failure. In fact, it makes you even more valuable as a business owner, even more prepared for another attempt.

Congratulations on choosing the entrepreneurship path. Thank you for choosing to use our guide to help you through the earliest, most precarious part of that journey: Start Up. As start-up guru Paul Graham wrote, "If you can just avoid dying, you get rich."

The wealth in your business – both financial and lifestyle – comes after you make it through the Start Up phase. On average, this takes a business three years: three years of riding the rollercoaster of emotions and cash flow until consistency sets in and you can feel relaxed.

Our goal in this guide is just the first year, the first 12 months. If you can "just avoid dying" in the first year, you are much closer to the third year, and then beyond. Of course, much of the advice and experience we share is designed to help you build your business for the long term right from the beginning.

We believe this guide will be a tool through all of your Start Up phase and beyond.

For now though, there is just one simple first step you need to make.

Decide to jump. Commit to no more thinking about starting a business, talking about the possibility with your friends, or going to events as an aspirational "wantrepreneur".

Commit to doing.

By Shan Naqvi & Jacob Aldridge

Mindset

Chapter 2

I was raised thinking that success meant finding a good job, but pretty consistently dabbled in entrepreneurship alongside whatever job I happened to have at the time. I left Facebook because I really wanted to have more freedom to be the mom I wanted to be to my kids – the time to participate in their school functions without worrying about taking time off of work.

"I also experienced some pretty serious health issues which triggered memories of losing my father at a young age and wanting to make sure that I was really focused on the important things in my life – my health, my kids, and my happiness.

"I believe it's important to be in charge of your future, and the best way to do that is to be in control of your income fully – through entrepreneurship. – **Meg Brunson**

"Running a business is challenging and can be downright frightening. It is essential to have great emotional intelligence skills (self-awareness, self-management, social awareness, and relationship management) in order to effectively work through the problems, obstacles, challenges, and issues that present themselves practically every day.

"Having a great attitude towards learning and growth and having compassion and empathy for others is the key." – **Paul Hoyt**

"Mindset is everything. Your Mindset is more important than the business you choose to do.

"Those 10 Steps to a proper Success and Wealth Mindset give you the tools you need to be successful. That proper Mindset and your Direction that comes from within will lead you to a Fulfilled Life doing work you love to do, and find Success by making money doing it.

Where people become disheartened or get discouraged is in the time it takes to achieve Success or a personal Dream. Just like the time it takes an acorn to become an oak tree, the same is true about becoming successful or achieving a Dream.

"A proper mindset will keep you on track to never, ever give up on yourself or your Dream. Remember, everything

By Shan Naqvi & Jacob Aldridge

was in the acorn in the beginning as it is with everyone." - **Richard Petenaude**

"Personally, I learned that I couldn't become my better self without knowing who I am in the first place. Many people try to better themselves through many resources and activities, but they don't know who they are. You can read, learn and do a lot of things but none of it will add value to your life until you know who you were created to be. You can even be an accomplished individual in your field and not know who you are." – **Louisa Jolanda**

The greatest business owners I [*NB: Unless otherwise noted, first person experience in this Guide is written by international business advisor Jacob Aldridge*] know didn't choose entrepreneurship because it "made sense" intellectually, or because they had a fear of missing out on the potential wealth that business can create.

They did it ... because they truly had no other choice. In their hearts and souls, they woke up as business owners and when they were employees their whole lives felt inconsistent, inauthentic.

That's entrepreneurship to me. I didn't choose it. It was just something I had to do – there was an energy in the universe that said "He Must! He Must!" It's something I see in other vocations as well, particularly a lot of creative arts like writing and acting.

And that's the mindset that gets me through the hard times. Consciously, I know there's an alternative to 'get a job' somewhere, but emotionally and realistically that's just not an option for me anymore. So I continue in business, because I must.

As you commence the entrepreneurship journey, it may surprise you that our guide focuses first on you, not your ideas, your business, or your customers. Yet this is what the research clearly demonstrates: ideas can pivot, business models evolve, and customers come and go over time. The North Star in your business, always, is you.

And your mindset, your emotional awareness, ripples outwards (quite dramatically at times) affecting every aspect of your business. When the boss has a bad day, the staff, the clients, the suppliers all notice it; and when you are on purpose feeling calm and with clarity of direction, that too gives confidence to all around you.

Practicing Mindfulness (and there are some wonderful free apps available) is a great habit to develop as a business owner. As a simple step though, choose to do this: Every morning before you go to work, and every evening when you finish for the day, ask yourself "How do I feel right now?"

Ask without judgement. Ask without needing to record the answer or even respond to it. By all means, if how you feel suggests that you need to change some aspect of your business or your life, then listen to your body's recommendation.

The simple act of checking in and acknowledging how you feel is often all that is needed to keep your energy up, your mindset clear, and your decisions on purpose.

Emotions of a Start-up

Chapter 3

Starting something new is a good thing. Be careful not to fall into the trap of always starting and never finishing, but on the whole starting something new will lead to positive things. If you are feeling nervous, scared, or timid when it comes to starting something, don't worry – everyone feels that way.

Embrace your feelings of doubt and push forward anyway. On the other side of fear is an expanded comfort zone and a fulfilling life. **– Jeff Davis**

I want you to think back to Day One in your business. Do you remember the day your business began? A majority of business owners I talk to it can actually still name the date, even if it was decades ago when they began their business.

And do you remember how you felt on that day? If you can, or maybe if you haven't even launched yet, the word I hear most often is "Excited". And it's true. I remember the first day I started my business, and I was excited like everyone else! Now, sometimes that excitement lasts for months, and sometimes it lasts for just a matter of minutes.

A graphic designer in London came up to me after a presentation once, to share her 'Excited' story. She had quit her job and finished on a Friday, and she vividly remembered the Monday morning when she started her own business.

She went into her kitchen – which, like so many start-up business owners, doubled as her office – and as she boiled her kettle to make a cup of tea (this was in England after all) she was completely overcome by excitement.

However, she told me, that excitement lasted just long enough for her to sit down at the kitchen table ... when it was replaced by panic and an overwhelming sense of dread and uncertainty. "What have I gotten myself into? I don't know how to run a business!"

These emotions for a start-up business owner are perfectly normal and natural. Knowing about them, especially beforehand, makes you a better leader. In the case of the graphic designer, she had been in business many years – at that point she had a business partner, staff, and a proper office in the City of London.

So her feelings weren't in any way an indication that her business would fail – they were just normal growing pains she had to experience.

That Start Up phase in business can be described as the journey from that initial excitement, the enthusiasm of having your own business or starting this new venture even if it's not your first business, and slowly having some of that joy dissipate until you found yourself in a 'Trough of Sorrow'.

This trough is a state of anxiety or uncertainty, of trying to determine whether or not this business is actually going to be viable. That initial excitement energy is fantastic because it gets you going.

You need it to get out of the bed in the morning in those early days of the business when there's a whole lot of inefficient, frantic, and overwhelming activity going on each day. Your wheels are spinning, but the car's not moving forward just yet!

You want to make sure you're putting in place the necessary things to get through that Trough of Sorrow as quickly as possible. The business lifecycle is a journey of speed bumps, hurdles, and brick walls — in that order. Speed bumps aren't that hard to get over, but you need to have some momentum and in the Start Up phase it's easy to get stuck.

To shift from Start Up into Scale Up, you shift your emotions from that excitement and that sorrow into Confidence that this business is going to work.

Moving into that "Confidence" is the first pivotal milestone for any start-up business owner. Nobody (no matter what they tell you) starts a business venture with confidence.

You start with hope, you start with some self-belief and hopefully belief in the market you are selling your product or service into. But it's only once people start to buy that real confidence comes your way.

Confidence will come eventually, and it's the emotion you need to make the investments that may be necessary to truly scale and grow, to being accelerating towards your vision now wheels are gaining traction.

So allow yourself to feel your feelings. And know that all of them, and especially in Start Up the progression from

The Start-Up Business Guide: 50 First Steps

Excitement to Overwhelm to Sorrow to Confidence is more than just normal – it's the sign your business is moving forward.

By Shan Naqvi & Jacob Aldridge

Don't Copy the Wrong Homework

Chapter 4

Do you think having a degree in anything is mandatory to start any business?

"It depends. For certain professions you need it. If you want to be a private brain surgeon, you better get one. Degree usually gives you credibility and relevant knowledge and experience.

But if you want to start a small product or service business, I think you learn more by working in one for some time, hanging around business owners, or even better, start one. Start small so you can get your hands on it and understand what it's all about.

Most degrees are very theoretical, and you end up with a lot of knowledge you won't use and $10,000x of debts.

I loved doing my degree in psychology, and it was a very important achievement in my life (I was the first one in my family to have a degree, let a lot in the second language). It has given me extra edge and credibility. But I also know that had I started my business instead, I'd be much further down the line today." - **Tomas Svitorka**

I have the privilege to speak at a number of conferences around the world, and I hear the question of "qualifications" a lot ... and even more often, I see people trying to grow their business by copying what works in someone else's.

So avoid this mistake before you even make it! Here's what often happens: you read a great case study on a website, or see an experienced entrepreneur speak (in person, or on YouTube), or maybe you took notes at a networking event.

And you think, "That's a great idea" so you walk back into your business and implement exactly what they did. More often than not, those great ideas, those practical suggestions that worked for someone else, prove to be a complete bust in your business, or worse.

Like the poetry major handing in math equations on his midterms, you copied the wrong homework. Let me show you how this happens, so you won't make the same mistake again.

By Shan Naqvi & Jacob Aldridge

The Lifecycle of Business

Every business goes through the same lifecycle – big or small, fast or slow, the journey is the same. How fast we move through may differ. And many – in fact, most – businesses don't survive the whole journey. For those that do, it's an emotional rollercoaster with speed bumps, hurdles and brick walls to navigate.

To help us understand – and therefore apply – this emotional journey better, I break it down into four separate cycles – Start Up, Scale Up, Step Up (when energy and profit sags), and Sell Up (when you choose to exit on your terms or go around again).

Within each of those smaller cycles, you can see a smaller journey – each of them can be broken into 3 distinct phases, investment, return on investment, and the phase when that investment has run its course.

As a business owner, you and your business are somewhere on this journey. If you're reading this guide, then you're likely in the Start Up phase or preparing to jump in (like Tomas recommends).

Every other business owner you talk to, listen to, or learn from is also somewhere on this journey. *But if they are not in the same place you are, then what works for them probably won't work for you!*

Let me give you the most common example, and it's the difference between the Start Up (when you need to focus on Revenue) and Scale Up (when you need to focus on Growth).

Most great business stories you hear are told by business owners in Scale Up – they're growing fast, feeling relaxed, and their business is nicely profitable.

My team run several dozen events each year, and like you I attend many more – how likely are you to go listen to a speaker who currently feels stuck in their business, is losing money, and is wondering whether this is all still worth it? Of course not, so these entrepreneurs never tell their story, and if your business is in one of those brick walls you'll walk away from every event thinking 'what am I doing so wrong?

Trust me, it's not you – it's them!

By Shan Naqvi & Jacob Aldridge

They tell you things like "invest in marketing", "take Fridays off", and "delegate responsibility to your team". Great advice, when you've established your business model and are scaling it up.

Terrible advice in Start Up. If you're before them on the lifecycle, you need to do things that don't scale – like working long hours, doing almost everything yourself, and squeezing in as much sales activity as you can muster.

If you don't, you'll join the 50% of businesses that fail in the first 3 years – they never make it to Scale Up ... in many cases, because they copied the wrong homework and acted like a Scale Up business before they were ready.

Top 3 Priorities

Chapter 5

With so much that *can* be done in your new business, and so much that *must* be done, it's hard sometimes to have clarity about what your top priorities are. What the authors of this guide found amazing, interviewing so many successful business owners and advisors and applying our own experience, is how the very best advisors are aligned on exactly your Top 3 Start Up Priorities.

We may use some slightly different language, but the key points are there. Take Paul Hoyt's top priorities:

1. Engaging with the marketplace as quickly as possible so you can learn the lessons that only the marketplace can teach you.
2. Building a great team
3. A relentless pursuit of financial stability – **Paul Hoyt**

And compare them with **Jacob Aldridge**'s:
1. Product-Market Fit
2. Business Model
3. Sustainable Sales

You can see the overlap. The first points are basically identical. The other two — having a great team and financial stability in Paul's words, and a solid business model and revenue stream in Jacob's — speak to the fundamental opportunity of entrepreneurship.

Are you building a team that can add value to the world, and profit to your company? The Start Up phase of business is the Revenue Phase. This is where it is most critical that you develop revenue strategy and systems for your business.

Let's explore how those 3 Priorities help you achieve that systemised revenue outcomes.

1. Product-Market

It's no good building a product that you love, if there isn't a target market for it. That's what we call 'A Solution in search of a Problem', and if you're not solving a problem (adding value to the customer) then you're not adding value to the world. You need to identify a target market and understand their pain, their problems, and how your solution, your product can help those clients.

These conversations are expanded in later chapters within this guide. Achieving a clear Product-Market Fit is normally an iterative process. So don't be disheartened if your first (or second, or twelfth) idea doesn't immediately excite your target market.

As long as you keep going back and forth in honest conversation with them, you will be evolving your product and your business to eventually help you to sell and deliver much more sustainably.

2. Business Model

You need to have the business processes in place so that when you take on a client, you can service and deliver to that client's expectations and do so in a in a systemized way that is at the very least almost profitable.

There's a saying in start-up businesses that "you need to do things that don't scale". Sometimes for your business model in the early stages of your journey you do need to do things that you're not going to be able to do forever – like handing out your personal phone number, or paying someone to manually complete steps that you know a machine or software will eventually be able to do.

You need to do these things just to prove that the product suits the market, and that your business model can work.

So it's OK as a start-up if your business model is metaphorically held together with duct tape. The more profitable your model can be sooner, the more free cash you will have to reinvest in your growth.

But there are plenty of businesses that aren't truly profitable until they begin to scale, and you can't scale if you don't win and keep those early customers.

3. Sustainable Sales

Can you generate new clients, new customers for your business on a sustainable way? A lot of start-up businesses and founders don't want to do sales. They think that their product is going to be so incredible that people are going to beat a path to their door. Unfortunately, that's not the reality of business.

Sales isn't a dirty word, particularly if you apply some of the Sales Model tips from later in this guide. Sales is about creating relationships, recognizing the value that you're delivering, and helping make sure your customers see that value as it applies to them.

The Start-Up Business Guide: 50 First Steps

Once you can articulate that value to win customers to your business, your focus needs to be on building the marketing and sales machine that's repeatable and scalable.

When this machines is working, it's truly magical to see: every month you can come in and put a dollar in the top of the machine, pull the business model lever, and watch the sales process flow until and a dollar and then some change comes out at the bottom ready to reinvest next month!

If you can build these three things – a clear product that has a clear market it fits into, the business model to deliver profitably, and then the sustainable sales to keep your business fed – that will give you the revenue that will give you the momentum you need to get through the Trough of Sorrow.

By Shan Naqvi & Jacob Aldridge

Target Market

Chapter 6

You've probably heard the refrain before: you can't be all things to all people. This is absolutely true in business – without a target market to focus on, your brand, marketing, and sales messages will be unable to cut through. And without being able to penetrate the hearts and minds of potential customers, not enough of them will buy.

Now, this doesn't mean the target market you choose when you begin is set for life. You will absolutely have opportunities to Pivot (Chapter 33) if need be, and eventually to expand and grow as you move from Start Up to Scale Up. But you won't make that progression if you don't get those initial customers.

So do you have a clear target market in mind for your business?

At this point you don't need to go into the detail of Brand Archetypes or Customer Personas - just a good idea of the industry your clients are in, the size of their business, who it is that this idea is going to help, or in the case of selling to consumers who they might be, where they might live, their buying habits and so on.

In validating your idea (Chapter 8), you will be asked to go and talk to people in this target market (yes, even if you have an online only business!).

You need to understand what pain those potential customers are experiencing and how your business can solve it. Asking these kind of questions is impossible if you think you can immediately start selling to 'everybody'.

Building a market is much harder than building a product or service, so it's important that you actually like and want to do business with your target customers. A great conversation we don't get to have often enough is when we meet entrepreneurial spirits who are driven to start a business, but have no idea what type of business to start.

My advice to people in this situation is to start with the Target Market. Think about who they want to work with as clients – then go and talk to a lot of those people about their lives, what they love and what challenges they face. Those challenges, if you can solve them, are your business idea.

This approach of talking to a lot of potential customers – doing market research, not sales, when you first start your business – is the best advice we can give. Because it's so much harder to convince people to spend their money with you than most people realise.

If you think you can just build a website and the customers will come, then you're going to be looking for a new job very soon.

Only by talking to people and asking them for their money will you truly understand what they value. Maybe that's similar to your current solution, maybe it's wildly different, but the chances of you having the perfect product or service from day one are very small. And that's OK!

Write down your Target Customers, in as much detail as you feel is relevant. Then also document what you believe their pain (and your solution) to be.

Value Proposition

Chapter 7

This chapter is based on the detailed discussion between Shan and the American author Steven E. Kuhn.

"Value proposition is the concept that people offering goods or services have to convince the customer that the good or service that they are offering is better than anything else out there. How did you establish this with your customers? I have clients, and we work on a series of outcomes starting with the mission, vision, personality and essence. Only then is a value proposition possible.

Too many people make up a website, make a colourful logo and create their digital footprint, then sit back and wait for the flood of traffic. They even get surprised when the flood of traffic doesn't magically materialise!

When your value proposition is crystal clear and actually presents a solution to a known problem for the specific demographic, sales are a result, not a goal. Unless you have a solid foundation in your complete message, you will always be the middle person who "wins some and loses some". To put it bluntly: nice words, a nice logo and all the marketing in the world will do less for you when people know you are solving a key problem. If you are not solving a problem, you may just be part of it in some way or the other.

Introducing (H.I.T)

H.I.T. Principles: Honesty + Transparency = Integrity.
   H.I.T. leads to Trust. Trust leads to manifesting what you want in life.

Honesty is being true to who you are and how you live. Transparency is communicating your honesty for anyone to observe. Integrity is the result and your ongoing reputation.

Benefits of living by H.I.T:

You have the clarity of who you are and exactly what you want in life.

You live an incredibly happy life where everyone seems to help you every step of the way. You naturally attract others who live by H.I.T., making life really easy and enjoyable.

When you operate under H.I.T. you get an authentic connection, significance, and true happiness. The Scarcity mindset evolves into an Abundance mindset. You will find yourselves being able to give value in the exact moment you are living.

You show up wholly and fully present for whatever comes, with no agenda, not trying to solve anything. You are simply there to provide value to elevate others.

In today's world, you see people following a trend because they are trying to be someone else and live through someone else. They're not living their true life because they don't know who they are.

HIT allows you to dig through the layers inward, rather than the outward following of trends. Stop wanting to be someone else. Start appreciating your true value, because you are worth a lot. When you believe "I can give back because I have value" then you empower yourself to dictate your own reality.

And that value in yourself as a business owner feeds into the value proposition of your business, whatever it may be, and the value you provide to your clients. Many business owners struggle to articulate their business's value proposition – not because they don't have a good product, but because they themselves feel they aren't worth more.

Do you truly value yourself and the value your business provides? It's normal to sometimes doubt that value – at times we all feel that we aren't good enough. Yet fundamentally, if you don't believe you're adding value through business then you will be unable to build a sustainable operation.

Validating Ideas

Chapter 8

One of the biggest mistakes of new business owners is thinking they know what the marketplace wants and will buy. They create a product or service offering and then try to find someone to sell it to, instead of finding a pain point in the market and creating a solution to match a very specific problem. – **Paul Hoyt**

"The number one reason for start-up failure is "no market need" - this comes from analysis by the CB Insights group looking into the reason behind hundreds of start-up failures.

Founders are often so convinced by their own perception of a problem they believe they are solving that they don't FIRST validate it in the market to determine a) the size of the potential market - it may be much smaller than what they think and b) if and how much people are willing to pay for a solution to the problem - many potential customers expect services to be offered for free these days with monetisation coming from sources other than them.

"Going through a rigorous proposition validation process with prospective customers will provide invaluable insights to reshape the proposition if required - it's always easier and cheaper to change the proposition prior to anything being actually built." – **Andrew Vorster**

This is a question we wish more start-ups and potential business owners would ask: do I actually have a good idea? Because all too often we see businesses fail because they built a solution in search of a problem, and when their Product didn't fit the Market ... they blamed the Market instead of taking responsibility.

Testing your start-up's new business idea is simple, but not necessarily easy. You need to commit to these 3 steps ... and truly listen to the response.

1) Clearly define your Target Customers
2) Document your understanding of Their Pain
3) Go and interview at least 10 (and preferably more) of these target clients and ask them whether they believe you have a good business idea.

You'll get 3 possible responses to that question. And you might be surprised to learn that the worst possible response is "Yes, that's a great idea". In Chapter 6 you completed the first two steps in this Validation process, and based on Chapter 7 you are hopefully feeling more confident in the value you can take out to that target market. Now the rubber hits the road!

You want to go and interview at least 10 of these target customers. You want to have an open conversation about their pain, and about how you are thinking you can solve that problem. Ideally, talk to at least 25 potential customers. This is very much an interview process.

You are asking questions, you are seeking their help, and you are looking to learn. **You are not under any circumstances to sell them anything in this conversation** (though you may schedule a return appointment with a different agenda).

Having talked about their pain and your solution, you can ask whether they feel yours is a good business idea. You will get one three responses:

1) **The first potential response you'll get is 'No'.** "No, I don't think this is a good business idea." Here's the thing: most first-time start-up business owners that I talk to think 'No' is the worst possible answer they could receive. But it's not. An honest

By Shan Naqvi & Jacob Aldridge

'No' sparks the conversation, it helps you advance your product development and product-market fit.

If it's a 'No', how it could be improved? How could you better understand their pain to solve their problem better? Do you need a whole new solution, or is it just a case of explaining and positioning your idea differently? All of those questions will improve your business.

2) The second potential response you will get is 'Yes'. "Yes, I think this is a good business idea."

'Yes' is actually the worst response you can receive! Because you can't be sure if "Yes, this is a great idea" is like the horrible outfit we all wore to our prom where mom said "Wow, you look fantastic!"

There's a lot of people out there who will say 'Yes' just to be nice. They don't want to hurt your feelings. Maybe they don't even know how they can give constructive criticism.

So when you go and talk with your 10 (or 25, or more) potential clients, you'll hear a lot of people saying 'Yes' ... and that does not help you with your business. You may invest a lot of time or hope in all those 'Yeses' that never actually turn into reality when you need people to buy.

3) **So what is the third possible response? The one you want to hear?** When you start talking to target customers about their pain and your solution, the only response that tells you have a good business idea is "Can I buy this now?" When you get to the end of the conversation, they're so excited by your idea that they don't want to discuss the details ... they want to know where they can send their money.

This response means they're committed, they are truly interested, and they're not just saying 'Yes' to look after your feelings. Business is not about having nice conversations.

Business is about truly solving pain and adding value – so if you think you've got a great idea, don't be afraid to find those target customers, have those interviews, and ask that question "Do you feel this is a good business idea?"

If the only responses you get are 'Yes' and 'No', then you need to keep refining your idea and keep having those meetings. Listen for the real answer. If you do that, you'll be head and shoulders above so many other start-ups we see that are struggling and don't know why, because they failed to do this one simple exercise.

<u>So this step is clear</u>: Do you have 10 people who represent your target market (or are knowledgeable about it) that you can go and talk with? If not, go and find them – you'll need to do this for Sales in the future anyway.

And don't be afraid to ask for the meeting. The magic word is 'Help' – as in, "I'm starting a business in your industry, and since you're an expert I would greatly appreciate your help.

Can I buy you a coffee / organise a 20 minute video call in the next two weeks?"

Structures

Chapter 9

As you start your business, you will need to make a decision about the Legal Structure/s that is most appropriate. Many founders spend too much time debating these options, *but* it can also be expensive to make changes later if you get it wrong.

The 3 contextual decisions you need to make are around Protection, Tax, and Investment. There are usually a range of options you can choose from, and having a good business accountant (Chapter 18) will help.

You will undoubtedly benefit from doing your own research, so we recommend doing some online searching for Business Structure options in your jurisdiction.

Protection is linked to the legal concept that Companies and Trusts are their own entities. If you operate a business yourself, all liabilities incurred by the business are attached to you personally. Should the business be sued, for example, all of your personal and family assets would be on the line.

If you own a company, however, you can separate the Company Assets from your Personal Assets. This is the origin of "Limited Liability" as a term (e.g., LLC) – simplistically, someone who sues the company is unable to pierce the corporate veil and go after your family's assets.

Specific rules apply, and they can vary extensively in different countries. In cases of malpractice, for example, you may retain personal liability; and for early-stage businesses, many banks or suppliers will 'request' you give personal guarantees anyway.

Partnership structures may appear to offer protection, but can be the worst of both worlds. In some cases, business partners are 'jointly and severally liable', meaning you are personally liable for any and all actions of your business partner.

Tax – every business owner's favourite topic!

"I pay whatever tax I am required to pay under the law, not a penny more, not a penny less, and the suggestion that I am trying to evade tax, which is what you're putting forward, I find highly offensive and I don't intend to cooperate with you in the blackening of my character.

"I am not evading tax in any way, shape or form. Now of course I am minimizing my tax and if anybody in this country doesn't minimize their tax they want their heads read because as a government I can tell you you're not spending it that well that we should be donating extra.

– Kerry Packer

Different business structures have different tax benefits. Mostly, these relate to Companies (which pay tax in their own right, and can retain profits for future investment rather than forcing the owners to pay tax at a high personal tax rate) and Trusts (which generally allow income or other tax benefits to be distributed unevenly to Beneficiaries, as a tax management strategy).

Understanding the difference between Income and Capital Gains Tax rates in your jurisdiction can also be relevant, and may impact you specifically if your business is Capital Gains heavy.

For example, there is a theory that Amazon has prioritised share price growth over company profits, because long term capital gains (when selling shares) in America are taxed at a lower rate than dividends would be.

As a start-up, you need to understand the return on investment you make from establishing a structure. For example, spending $1,500 to establish a structure may not be necessary if you don't yet have any revenue.

And critically, never make a business decision solely for tax purposes. Make it a relevant factor, because the less tax you pay the more you have to reinvest. But founders who chase the lowest tax payments often do it at the expense of actual business success – after all, the only guaranteed way to pay no tax is to lose lots of money every year!

Investment is a broad way of asking if you plan to have at start-up, or in the future, business partners or investors. As the name suggests, you're not able to take investors if you're a sole operator or sole trader! You will need to establish some kind of corporate structure. The specifics of your options are outside the scope of this guide.

If you hope or plan to take on investors in the future, make sure your accountant knows this and has experience with businesses that have done so successfully.

What Business Structure have you chosen?

Brand and Name

Chapter 10

One of the most exciting – and daunting – aspects of a start-up business is choosing your name and brand. We want you to enjoy this process – but don't waste time here, because we guarantee that some aspects of your brand and marketing will appal you in a very short space of time!

First, some definitions. Your Brand is **not** your Name or Logo. Both of those elements are important, but your Brand is the higher-level concept that sits behind it. Some nice ways we've heard Brand described:
- Brand is what makes you famous (in your market)
- Brand is how people describe you when you're not in the room

What is brand?

Be careful not to confuse this Brand with your Brand*ing*. Your branding is the visual representation of your brand, through colours, fonts, key messages and collateral. You need your branding to be consistent across different mediums and congruent with your Brand message, but don't confuse the messenger for the message.

Lastly, there are related concepts like your 'Elevator Pitch', 'Unique Selling Proposition', and 'Brand Promise'. We'll give you a useful tool for creating this, but again these are just one small part of your Brand and it's important to be flexible with them.

What is brand promise?

Have you ever found yourself stuck at a function, gasping like a goldfish because someone has asked you the 'What do you do?' question? It can be tricky to be put on the spot, having to find the fine line between being specific (but boring) and being exciting ('we stimulate synergies for revolutionary business models') but ridiculously vague.

There's no benefit in having a single, scripted elevator pitch or positioning statement - how you describe your business at a family barbecue needs to be different to how you introduce yourself on stage as the industry keynote.

But you want consistency - to make your life easier, and to ensure that every member of your team is describing what you do and who you do it for in the same manner.

Here's the super-simple (and therefore effective) Brand Promise framework we use, whether you're driving limousines, coaching entrepreneurs, or (ahem) stimulating synergies.

We like to use the term 'Brand Promise' because it links this conversation to two key elements: your bigger overall Brand strategy and the Promise that you make your customers at every step through the customer journey (see Chapter 37).

We break it down into these five simple questions (though feel free to personalize these to create your own unique brand promise structure).

1) **What do you do?** *In a Technical sense e.g., I'm a business coach*
2) **Who do you do it for?** *This is your Ideal client, e.g. For B2B founders with 12 to 96 staff*
3) **What is their pain point?** *Feelings are good here e.g., Who feel they've reached the limits of their leadership ability*
4) **What DON'T you do?** *So your team etc. are clear e.g., We don't give financial advice*

5) **What's your secret sauce?** *This is the hook e.g., my methodology gives them the courage to grow faster and delivers a 500% return on investment*

You'd be surprised how many business founders struggle to actually answer that **first question** directly! Here's a common example, from a group workshop I ran once.

I picked on somebody in the audience and asked "What do you do?" He replied, "We give Brides an excellent experience." "That's great, and that sounds nice and that's helpful. But what is it you do?"

"Well you know, we set clear expectations with Brides on their wedding day. And we make sure they've got no stress." I said again, "That's fantastic, that sounds really helpful. But **what is it that you do?**" Can you believe this went back and forth three or four more times, until he finally acknowledged that "he was a limousine business"?

So all of those other elements were absolutely true: that was a big part of his Brand. The value that he delivered to his clients was that he would be there on the biggest day of their life. But he needed to make sure he actually told them what they did, because he could well have been a florist, or an event manager, or a caterer. None of that came through until he explained "we rent limousines for brides".

Questions 2 and 3 are about your ideal client and their pain points, which of course you answered in Chapter 6 and tested with real live interviews in Chapter 8. These are critical parts of your Brand Promise, because ultimate your business is not about you – it's about your clients.

Question 4 is optional for a start-up, when you're still testing the market and evolving what you do. However, it is important for you and your team to understand what it is you don't do because it can be tempting to start promising that you'll do anything for anybody.

Articulating the things that you don't do helps focus your Brand Promise, and it's that focus that creates cut through to your target market.

The last question is where you can start to have a little bit of fun: what is it about your process, your methodology, your business that makes it special? For our limousine driver, "We drive limousines for brides who want to make sure that nothing goes wrong on the most important day of their life. Our process ensures that they are fully looked after and never have to worry about where the car is and where they're going to next."

Practice these for yourself, in particular by sharing them with real people and seeing their response. Do they understand what you do? Do they understand who would benefit from working with you?

And, most importantly if they're within your target market: does this description make them want to learn more ... or buy immediately?

Name

A pivotal question in the life of your start-up: What is your Business Name going to be? Some key considerations:

1) Do you need a separate business name?

Plenty of consultants and professional services firms simply use the name of their founder or partners. The long tradition of this naming approach can immediately add professionalism and credibility – and also saves you having to conjure something more original or exotic.

2) Can you use a basic descriptor?

At the first level of original business names, you can combine a relevant descriptor with your industry or product. Take an adjective, run it through an online synonym search, and play around with what you like: is "Optimal Lawyers" better sounding to you than "Prime Family Law"?

3) Get Creative

That synonym search can also be a base for being inventive – swap vowels, combine sounds, invent whole new words. "Optimus Prime Lawyers" has a ring to it!

4) Then Review the Online Real Estate

Which brings us to the final (well, you'll want to test it as well) and potentially most frustrating aspect of naming your business: checking available company names, web domains, and social media handles.

In the good old days of life before 1998, you really only had to have a unique name in your local geography (unless or until you wanted to become a multinational). There could be "Optimus Prime Lawyers" in every State, and it wouldn't necessarily affect you in your target market.

Today, your dream name might be ruined because a Solopreneur in Reykjavik has already registered your website name! So iterating between this Chapter and the next may help you identify a name that you can actually 'own'.

5) Brand

What can you actually do to make your brand message famous? In future chapters we will explore your marketing strategy (if you even need one); for now, what is your focus?

We ignore so much of the advertising that hits us today. To cut-through, you need to access our brains and leverage neuromarketing to make an impact and be remembered. The specific approach we recommend is Brand Archetypes.

We as humans are hard-wired, pattern-recognition machines. If you've seen any of the *Star Wars* movies you know that when somebody is dressed in white they're the good guy and when somebody shows up in black they're the bad guy.

Our brain connects those messages on such a fundamental level that the filmmaker doesn't need to explain it anymore. Brand Archetypes takes that power, aligning your company Brand with some fundamental human drives.

The 12 Archetypes we leverage are those developed by the firm Brandonian

- Ruler
- Creator
- Sage
- Innocent
- Explorer
- Rebel
- Hero
- Magician
- Jester
- Commoner
- Lover
- Caregiver

Your Brand aligns with one of these specifically. The reason we recommend the Brandonian system – unlike others that simply have a list – is that their system maps each of the 12 Archetypes against the two axes of human desire:

Risk versus Stability, and *Belonging versus Independence.*

All of us are motivated by those four factors, despite the conflicting nature of each axis.

Your Brand thus takes a position on both, the combination of which defines your specific Archetype which all of your messaging can leverage to cut-through.

Not sure which of the 12 is right for you? Make sure you register on our website for the bonus features to this Start-up Guide, which includes a free online Brandonian Brand Diagnostic.

What's your Brand Promise? Do you love your Business Name? And are you clear what you represent in the market?

Start-up Digital Footprint

Chapter 11

Later in this Guide we will talk about building your Marketing Strategy and how important it is to have a clear and documented plan for finding your earliest customers. You probably don't want to wait that long to establish a digital footprint, however!

So how can you quickly and effectively 'go digital' (especially if you have a digital business selling your products or services online)?

Setting up your online presence is an important early step. Let me share some creative tools with you to set up your online business and get you started.

Setting up a Social Media Page on different platform

- Facebook is a social media platform that almost everyone uses. Facebook has proved to be the most powerful platform to interact with people. And it makes sense to have a relationship with people in your industry. Getting a Facebook page can also help you with referrals, as it is much easier to refer

people to a website than to try to explain the importance that another person can give.
- LinkedIn is a great online forum to help you connect with professionals. It is used to build a powerful network, and can also be extremely valuable over time as people change jobs, or industries, and you are able to keep in touch with them.
- Pinterest is a social media platform and mobile application that primarily uses images and, at a smaller level, GIFs and videos. It can be great for certain B2C demographics, but less so for business owners if they are your target market.
- Twitter can be a powerful tool for conversations and customer feedback, but it's harder to have client discovery on the platform because the volume of the short messages (and the secretive algorithm for displaying your tweets to your followers) means your Tweets are very quickly buried.
- Instagram, like Pinterest, is an excellent way to show off a visual business, and is more popular.

Of course, the social media space is always changing. In general, you don't want to spend too much time on a brand-new social media platform (like **Snap chat** or **TikTok**) unless you really enjoy being at the cutting edge.

Many small business owners invested time into **Google+, Myspace, Meerkat,** and so on – time which they would have better spent on their own blog of email database.

Most business owners are worried about playing with more than one or two social media networks, and that's a wise concern. You are much better off selecting two from the list where your target customers spend time and engaging with that network fully, then you are trying to have a limited profile across all of them

Setting up your website

Your website is your personal web page that might look a lot more professional than your social media presence. No matter how popular you are on social media, you always want your own Website and your own Database.

I've seen Facebook accounts with 600,000 Followers deleted for a minor rules breach: do not build your business on someone else's land. Let me show you some of the basic steps to set up a website.

Domain: When you set up a website for your company, registering a domain is the first and most important part of it. A domain name usually costs about $8 dollars a year, though this can be more if you want a geographic specific (e.g., ".co.uk") or specialty TLD (like ".tv"). Start searching for a domain to have your own website at www.yourbusinessname.com.

In general, you always want both the ".com" and the country-specific domain for any markets you want to be in. As a start-up, you will still only have one website, but the other domains will "redirect" to that site in case a prospect types in the wrong address.

Generally, it's wise to avoid domains that have hyphens or some of the newer TLDs (like ".rodeo" – yes that really exists). If you can't buy the ".com" or (which is also OK) the country specific domain where you are based, that means someone else owns that domain … and as a result, they have some control over how your company is perceived.

The most common workarounds if you have a great business name but can't get the right domain: add a prefix like "get", "the", or "real" (Dropbox was originally getdropbox.com until they had enough money and profile to buy Dropbox.com) or a suffix like "business", or even just the name of your industry or geographic area. Alternatively, a few TLDs have become widely known and so run less of a risk in confusing your prospective clients: ".tv" (Tuvalu) and ".io" (The British Indian Ocean Territory) are good examples.

Hosting: You need a contract with a company to host your website. This is similar to saving your data on your computer. Hosting accounts can cost as little as $2-5 a month, though this will increase if you want features like automatic backups or when you start getting a lot more traffic to your site.

Design: Once you have bought your domain and hosting, how do you design and set up your website? Your first option is to pay someone to build your website for you. This requires money, and will still involve a lot of your time so don't think it's 100% outsourced.

Usually it creates a better looking website that you can keep for longer; most self-built business websites will need replacing by a professional (or rebuilding yourself) every year or two.

By Shan Naqvi & Jacob Aldridge

At Start Up, unless you need to sell products and take money online, you probably only need a 'brochureware' site with a blog that you can update yourself without paying a developer ongoing. It's called 'brochureware' because, like a printed brochure, the information won't change very often.

The essential pages are "Home", "About Us / Meet the Team", and perhaps "Our Services / Can We help you?"

Expect to pay $1,500 for a bare bones website (you might get lucky paying less than that; or you may give money to someone inexperienced who wastes your time and builds something ugly) and up to $5,000 for a professionally-styled website that maybe has a few more pages.

It's certainly possible to pay more than that, but unless you need some additional functionality, as a start-up your money is probably better invested elsewhere.

WordPress is content management software that can help you create efficient and professional websites with no programming skills. Neither of us are affiliated with WordPress, but it's the software we both used (even before we met each other) because of its low cost, high quality, and reliability.

Many professionals use WordPress, which means it can be a good option if you outsource the initial build but want to do future updates and blogs yourself. If you are building your own website (which both of us did at first), then WordPress is highly recommended. With thousands of free themes and plugins, you can create a stunning, professional website in an hour or so.

So now: how do you drive traffic to your beautiful website, get followers on social media, or begin to pay for advertising? All of this (and more) is covered in the Marketing Strategy steps from Chapter 38.

There's certainly more than one Step in this Chapter. As a start: make sure your website is being built professionally on the best domain you can source; and pick the two social media channels your target market (and you) are most likely to spend time on and begin having conversations there.

By Shan Naqvi & Jacob Aldridge

Product

Chapter 12

Throughout this guide, we use the words 'Product' and 'Service' largely interchangeably. This is because the basic lessons in business apply universally, whether you are manufacturing widgets in China and selling them into the USA, or whether you are a professional services business working on an hourly rate.

For every business, having the right Product or mix of Products is essential. After all, without a product to sell … you don't have a business.

"It must be something you love doing and have huge passion for. Running a business is hard, and if you don't like what you're doing, you won't last. You might as well get a job (you don't like). At least you'll have more financial security.

"There must be a need for your product or service out there. You may be passionate about doing spaghetti sculptures, but if no one want's one, you won't make a business out of it." - **Tomas Svitorka**

"Start a business that you are passionate about and know about.

"If you don't know anything about aerospace engineering and have no passion for it and you decide to start an aerospace company because you read a story that people are getting rich off of it, you will most likely NOT be successful. Do what you know!" - **Jeet Benerjee**

Having said that, there are some key differences between Product and Service businesses. If you're unsure about which business idea to pursue, or are already thinking about how to expand your mix of products to include both Products and Services, then it's helpful to understand those differences.

"There are two huge differences. First, a product company takes a lot longer and requires a much bigger investment of time and money to reach profitability. Many companies spend a year and $250,000 only to find out that the market doesn't want to buy their products in enough quantity or at a high enough price for the company to be profitable. Then they lose everything.

"Services businesses can be started overnight. You just decide what you want to sell and start selling it.

"The other huge difference is in the value of the company. A product company with $10,000,000 in revenues is worth a lot more than a service business with the same revenue. The product company will have inventory and likely some intellectual property.

"With the service business, all of the employees could walk out the door tomorrow and the investor would be left with nothing. That's why it is very difficult for a service business to raise capital." – **Paul Hoyt**

Pricing

Chapter 13

Your potential clients must be able to pay your price.
- **Tomas Svitorka**

Your pricing starts with a question about one of Jacob's favourite topics: beer. Imagine that you've hosted an amazing party where everyone's drinking bottled beer. You wake up the next morning a little bit sore, wander into the kitchen, and open up the fridge to see how many beers are left. My question is this: what's the perfect number of beers that you will find in the fridge?

Most people think "Zero" is the perfect number. "If we had no beers left, then that's a fantastic sign, perfect number". BUT. The problem with "zero beers left" is that you're not sure how many people *wanted* more beer, but weren't able to drink because there were no more left.

The perfect number of beers is "One". If there's one beer left, then that means everybody had exactly the amount they needed. And you didn't overprovide or over-cater for that party.

So, what the heck does having one beer left have to do with pricing? It relates to your conversion rate – what percentage of prospects do you convert into paying clients. If you're converting every single client that you sell to, then almost certainly your prices are too low.

Just like people miss out on beers if you run out of beers, your business is missing out on revenue (extra revenue that would go straight to your bottom line, profit), because you're not priced appropriately.

As a start-up, you need to focus on the value that you deliver to your customers, absolutely. Just make sure that you're pricing yourself accordingly. Most founders fear pricing themselves too high, because they will lose clients (or convert far fewer). At some point this is true – if your prices were 50% higher, you might have 0% of the clients.

But if your price was 20% higher, and only 5% fewer prospects converted, your business would be much better off – higher gross profit margins, and either more revenue or the same revenue for less work.

So how do you set your prices correctly?

Firstly, make sure you are valuing yourself. This is the mindset and emotional rollercoaster we talked about right at the beginning of this guide. You bring value to the world: make sure you price you value accordingly, and don't sell yourself short.

One model we recommend for start-ups who are unsure (where this is possible) is to make sure your pricing isn't published and just test and increase your prices with every new client until people start saying no.

One business we worked with had this issue. They were charging $5,000 for a business analysis, and while they felt it was "too cheap" they weren't sure what the right price was. So I set the challenge: from now on, put the price up by $1,000 for each new prospect until somebody says no.

The first "No" they received was at $14,000! Now they sell the service for $13,500 – the clients still receive excellent value, and can demonstrate a return on their investment. The business can do half as many projects each month, and still earn more money.

By Shan Naqvi & Jacob Aldridge

What are your prices? Why did you set the price at that level? How can you test that your price is the optimal balance delivering value to your clients as well as your business?

Business Model

Chapter 14

Business model innovation is the greatest differentiator in both product and service orientated businesses. There is always multiple ways to deliver the same outcome - consideration should be given to scalability and profitability of each along with the associated risks. **– Andrew Vorster**

Many business owners, once they begin their early days, want to take all the responsibility on their own. I'm not saying that taking responsibility is bad – it's one of the most important aspects of being a successful business owner.

But so too is knowing when to transfer responsibility, and not do all their work on your own. You may be tempted, because of your passion of your lack of cash, to want to do it all.

You want to build your own website, which can be rewarding but takes a lot of time to learn, particularly when you're a non-tech person who doesn't know their CSS from their ASS.

By Shan Naqvi & Jacob Aldridge

You want to design your own logo, which takes a long time to learn. And when you're not an artist or a creative person, that's a lot more difficult.

There was a time when I started my business, and then I started doing all these things on my own, and it was so hard for me to learn all these things. Sometimes I just couldn't do that, and in trying to do that I was holding my whole business model back.

Let me think about the five main things I've learned so far ... and I think you're expected to do if you don't want to struggle to get started.

1) **The first thing is to start a business you're actually excited about.** Don't just look at Bill Gates and start making a software company, even though you don't know how to program and you hate to code.

    Remember, why are you starting a business not working a job? Because you want to be a master of your own life doing what you want to do. Without passion, or at least some interest and aptitude, it's impossible to start a business.

For 'get rich quick' schemes or ideas outside your areas of interest, you might find success in your first days. But later, you'll find yourself frustrated and you'll find yourself in trouble because your business model will depend on you doing work you don't care to do.

2) **Don't try to learn everything and do it on your own.** If you're obviously a writer, go and learn about WordPress, but if you have a company in conventional terms then just concentrate on what you really ought to do.

If you start a coaching business and then spend most of your days learning how to build a website, then really you're building two businesses – the coaching business and the website building business. You're spreading yourself too thin, and you won't achieve the volume you need to succeed.

Outsource or recruit the right people for the right jobs. The rise of office workers is almost over, and the Internet is so strong that you can recruit anyone anywhere in the world. You may do this to find great people who are cheaper (helpful in the beginning of a start-up) or it may just be that the best person to help you lives somewhere else.

After all, if you're sitting in a town of 10,000 people or a city of 1,000,000 ... what's the chance that the best candidate from 7,500,000,000 humans alive today happens to live in the same location?

3) **Pay some of the capital.** When start-ups reach out to me, the first thing they talk about is funding. They don't want to pay anything, they don't believe they can pay anything, and yet they still want to do business.

While it's possible this could work, and some incredible partnerships (see Chapters 24 and 25) have begun this way, equity is expensive, owing favours can be expensive, and so wheeling and dealing to get something for nothing is usually not the perfect thing to do.

You've got to invest in your business: it's not just money, it's time too. You've got to make it work. And sure, that's a huge responsibility. As a founder, you've got to take all the responsibilities and risks.

If you're disappointed to hear this, please move on to a regular job.

4) **Try to make some of your own products.** Now I know it's possible that you can do a great deal of business by selling other goods, and make a massive amount of money as a distributor or a marketplace (like Alibaba or Amazon). But this isn't as important as making your own goods.

Selling your own brand means you can control the product and receive more of the profits. OK, you may begin re-selling someone else's creation, but a product you don't 'own' is a commodity and that means a race to the bottom on prices.

5) **Personal growth.** Now you've got to wonder why I'm talking about personal growth here that sounds like a life coaching kind of thing to you, right.

Let me tell you that this is very important to you. I see a lot of start-ups sitting on the chair all the time in front of the screen, and they're going to fail badly because of disappointment and anxiety, natural start-up emotions that overwhelm you because you're stuck on your own.

Practice self-care rituals, right from the beginning of your business. Meditation and Mindfulness are free and take minutes a day. Do some exercise, please? Eat healthy. Sleep well.

Some of these things may feel like they're costing you time and money, but the actual outcome is that you are more and more productive.

At its simplest form:

Business Model = Volume x Profit

In the early days, you want to get the balance right, which is why we talk about target market (Volume) and pricing (Profit). Fairly quickly though, you'll need to pick one of these to prioritise.

Do you focus on Volume: making sure you profit on every sale, but keeping those profit margins low in order to win more business?

Of do you focus on Profit: probably selling fewer products or services, but with a profit margin (usually supported by a Brand and Sales system) that's much higher?

This is one of the core questions you as a business owner need to decide, and to continually re-assess. When you're doing everything on your own, worrying about the small stuff, and running yourself into exhaustion, then you're missing the big picture: what's the business you're actually building?

What's your Business Model? Do you have a team to help, or not? Are you prioritising your sustainable health? And which is more important to you in the year ahead: Volume, Profit, or finding the initial balance?

By Shan Naqvi & Jacob Aldridge

Break Even Formula

Chapter 15

When starting and growing a business, there are many critical numbers: your revenue, your profit margin, and how much cash you have in the bank are three figures that immediately come to mind!

And when I talk to existing business owners, they are usually clear about those pieces of financial information. A number that they're less clear about – but which is just as important – is their Break-Even Point on a monthly basis.

In other words, do you know how much money your business needs to generate this month in order to Break Even (i.e., cover all of your expenses, so neither losing money nor making a profit)?

Knowing this figure gives you a specific target when planning any of your revenue or growth plans. If you know how much the business costs to run each month, then you have the first monthly sales goal for example.

If you're not yet in business, you might think this is an easy figure to calculate, but the reality is that some of your monthly expenses are fixed and some are variable – they are linked to how much revenue you bring in.

In this chapter, I combine that information to share with you the formula to help a business understand where that Break Even Point is and therefore what your formula is for profit.

Break even = Fixed Costs / Gross Profit Margin %

Step 1) First, you need to understand your business's Fixed Costs. These are the expenses you have to pay no matter what - things like your rent, most of your staff, a lot of overheads, leases, software and so on.

These are going to be the same each month same regardless of whether you sell a dime's worth of actual business services or you sell a million bucks' worth!

(This figure is sometimes called "the cost of opening the doors". Just by opening the doors to your business each month, you are committing to this amount of expenses.)

Step 2) Once you understand those Fixed Costs, you then need to separate out the Variable Costs within your business. These are costs that you will only incur when you sell your product or service – almost by definition they are a percentage of your revenue.

As a side note, I say *almost* by definition because if you find that your Variable Costs in and of themselves exceed the actual revenue that you generate from that product then you've got a dog of a business!

That means it costs you more to sell your product than you bring in in revenue, which means you're going out of business backwards.

I'm not a believer in "Loss Leaders". I can certainly understand that some products or services may have a lower margin, but you don't want to create a business where for every dollar of revenue you generate your Variable Costs are more than a dollar.

Partly, this is because the Variable Costs are going to sit on top of the Fixed Costs, those overheads that you can't get out of and have to pay every month regardless.

While there are exceptions for well-funded venture capital companies, again this is risky for the average start-up business founder. Eventually, you want your business to turn a profit.

Once you know your Fixed Costs and Variable Costs, you can project your revenue and profit forecasts much more accurately. Your Variable Costs are a percentage of revenue, so you can start to calculate what extra Variable Costs you will incur for every extra dollar of Revenue.

Some businesses may have a Variable Costs of just one or two cents on the dollar – they're heavy on fixed overheads like professional staff who are paid a salary no matter what. Some business have Variable Costs that are much higher – they're selling a product at a low margin like retailers.

If your financial reports, especially your Profit and Loss Statement does not separate out Fixed and Variable Costs then you will struggle to discover (which is the point of this chapter) where exactly your Break-Even Point is.

Step 3) This is the easiest step! To calculate your 'Gross Profit Margin', just subtract your Variable Cost Percentage from 100%.

If your Variable Costs are 60% of your Revenue ... then your Gross Profit Margin is 40% (100% - 60%).

Step 4) Because your Break-Even Point is calculated by adding the Variable Costs on top of the Fixed Costs, and working out where Revenue crosses the line.

Revenue starts at $0. Fixed Costs starts somewhere higher – say $10,000. Variable Costs also start at $0 (if you have $0 revenue), but they get added on top of the Fixed Costs.

So say your Variable Costs are 60% and you generate $10,000 worth of Revenue. This means your total costs for the month are $24,000 - $10,000 in Fixed Costs and $4,000 (40% of the $10,000 Revenue) in Variable Costs. Your Revenue is climbing, but so is the total amount of your expenses.

Your Break-Even Point is where the Revenue line would cross those Expenses. In this example:

Break even = Fixed Costs / Gross Profit Margin %

Break Even = $10,000 divided by 40%
Break Even = $25,000

You need to generate $25,000 each month in order to break even.

(And you can double check this math. If you did $25,000 in revenue then your Variable Costs would be $15,000 (60% of $25,000). That would leave you with $10,000 left, which is used to cover your Fixed Costs.)

Everything that your business generates over and above that Break-Even Point is profit. This is the situation where all of the Fixed Costs have been met, where you have exceeded the runway on those Variable Costs and moving forward you continue to grow the margin as a percentage over the top.

As you can see, understanding where your break-even point is gives you a specific target each month. You ideally want to hit that target as early as possible in the month, so that you can exceed and build out that profit.

For every $1 of revenue above Break Even Point, you are creating a Net Profit (i.e., the money you get to 'keep') equal to the Gross Profit – it goes 'straight to the bottom line'.

As a final caveat, there are other ways of calculating this, and there are other more complicated elements like knowing your 'Cash Break-Even Point'. As we will see in a later chapter, a good accountant will always pay for themselves when it comes to helping you to grow your business and may be useful in calculating a more complicated model that provides you with more accurate data.

Hopefully, however, you've seen how just using those three simple elements (Fixed Costs, Variable Costs, and Revenue) can help you calculate this number for yourself and ensure you consistently have that desirable fourth element: **Net Profit!**

RNR Colors: Roles 'n' Responsibilities for Rest 'n' Recuperation

Chapter 16

I use a lot of colour in my business and when coaching and training other business owners. And the colours I use are quite deliberate – a specific set of colour choices that are part of my overall business system, which you're reading about in this guide as a way to help start-up and growth entrepreneurs to run better businesses.

The most powerful way my clients take these colours and use them in their everyday life, is by colour-coding their diaries or schedules. Adding colour adds meaning, and the outcome is a more focused use of your time, and better team support.

You can use whatever colours you want – these are the ones that work for me and my clients.

Here's one of the big reasons great ideas fail in small business – you. Specifically, you become a bottleneck in your business. Too many key decisions come through you, which means you don't have enough time to work on the things that really matter.

By Shan Naqvi & Jacob Aldridge

In Australia 'You're flat out like a lizard drinking'; in America 'You're too busy fighting alligators to drain the swamp'; in my world, 'You're stuck in the Blue and Red when you really need to be in the Black and Green'.

What do I mean by that? Well if you think about every area of your business, every task, we can group them into 1 of these 4 categories, which we colour code to make it more meaningful and memorable.

In the Black you have Asset and Equity building tasks – like setting the Vision for your business, understanding Valuation drivers, financial planning and asset protection.

In the Green you have Growth activity – building a capacity plan, designing a Brand & Marketing strategy, new product development and so on.

In the Blue are your short-term Revenue tasks – sales, managing workflows, servicing clients.

And in the Red are the Overheads – administration, invoicing, facilities management.

You did NOT start this business to spend half your time on invoicing and facilities management! Yet when I ask most business owners to break down their month, they almost always have way too much time in the Blue and Red tasks and not enough in the Black and Green ... even though the Black and Green are the areas that ignite their passion.

Your time is the single most valuable resource your business has, and therefore its most valuable investment. Stop investing it in short term activities!

Learn to hand over responsibilities and decision-making to your team, to free you up to invest more time where you can get the greatest return.

How do you do that?

First, understand where you are currently investing your time. What Percentage of your week or month is split across those four colours, Black | Green | Blue | Red?

If you're not sure, colour-code your diary and/or task list for 2 weeks to find out. Based on my experience, you'll be surprised where your time actually goes – and many of my clients who complete this exercise begin colour-coding their diary permanently, and asking their team to do the same.

Secondly, once you know where your time is currently going, ask yourself where you WANT to be investing your time. (Again, as a percentage across Black | Green | Blue | Red).

What dollar value would that change in investment create? I've seen many small business owners calculate their Black and Green time at $1,000s per hour, which makes it a lot easier to hand over the $25/hr. admin tasks they're doing.

It's important at this point to note that none of the four colours are more important or more valuable than the others. It's also true that many start-up businesses fail because they fail to build the right systems in the Red – if you don't have the right contracts and billing processes, you won't survive in business no matter how great the vision and strategy.

But you can OUTSOURCE or RECRUIT people to do those tasks, and frankly the people you employ are likely much better at those tasks that you are. This may feel difficult in the early stages of your business, when incoming cash is tight.

Recognise that every hour you don't have to do Red Admin is another hour you can invest in Blue Revenue, Green Marketing and so on.

The third and final question, when looking at the difference between your time now and where you want it to be, is 'What needs to change to make that happen?'

Let Go to Grow, and invest some time in a three month Roles & Responsibilities project where you can gradually hand over the harder tasks or recruit / outsource the right people to take them off your hands.

We're here to give you a better business system that truly empowers your bright ideas. Why shouldn't your business have a colourful future?

By Shan Naqvi & Jacob Aldridge

Work Flows

Chapter 17

You can definitely optimise a start-up business too soon. Especially if it's just you, or only a small team, then spending too much time trying to find the 'perfect' way to work can suck time and money away from those more important revenue-generating activities.

Having said that, as you win more clients and the business starts to grow, you want to ensure that you (and your team) are consistently delivering your product or service to the standard your clients are expecting. And clear, documented Workflows are a valuable part of making that happen (and saving you the time having to micro-manage your team).

If you've ever had a situation where members of your team (in your business, or previous jobs) aren't sure who does what in what order then you need to get this documented. The process in this chapter is designed to be colourful so it can be clearly communicated to you, your team, and potentially even your clients so that they know the process they're going through to get to their outcome!

If you like, you can use the four colours we discussed in the previous Chapter to separate out the different areas of your business: Black for Wealth, Green for Growth, Blue for Revenue, and Red for Admin.

By colour-coding each step, you can very quickly see a workflow process that bounces between different colours – and this is a key sign of inefficiency, as the different colours usually have different mindsets or different team members completing them.

The colours also mean the end result, a documented Workflow diagram, is a visual piece of meaningful art that you can even hang on the wall of your workspace. That's quite an improvement over something that's bland and done with triangles in Microsoft Word.

The other approach we use to uncover Workflow inefficiencies is to map the steps using 'Swim Lanes'. Every role in the business (and as the Founder, you may have multiple roles, so it's OK to separate out Marketing, Sales, Delivery, Accounting even if you wear all those hats for now) takes its own lane on your diagram.

The steps in the Workflow then move between those different lanes as the process or client moves from one functional area of your business to another.

Not sure which Workflow to do first? Mapping the process from Sales through your Delivery team (Workshop, Studio, Factory, Office etc.) is the most common one, and the most valuable for getting right.

You start creating this Workflow by asking (yourself, or your team) "What happens when a lead comes in to our business?" This box "Lead Comes In" goes at the top left of your diagram … and yes, I encourage doing this exercise visually on a whiteboard to larger sheet of paper!

Chances are, that Lead goes to the sales team, and maybe the salesperson makes a phone call. In the 'Sales' swim lane we create a box for 'Phone Call', and we draw an arrow to show the connection between the two.

Then you want to ask, what happens next? If you as a business owner want to facilitate the conversation, then that's a question you'll get to ask a lot: "OK, then what happens next?" This allows you to walk through every step along the sales process, likely ending with a happy client (are you asking for referrals or reviews?) and a notification to the accounts person.

In a small business you can actually get the entire Workflow onto a single sheet of paper; the larger your business grows, the more you need to break down some of those Workflows into different areas in the business like sales, a factory particularly in a larger manufacturing business, or accounting and finance who can often get to a lot of detail around the different steps that those individuals take.

Within a business that's got multiple people (and especially multiple business partners doing similar work, like a professional services firm) you've got to break it down even further.

The level of detail in your workflow is the level of detail that is right for you for your business – so it's not as simple as just copying what another business in your industry does. Make it your own, and by asking those questions you ensure that documenting your current Workflow is not a lengthy process.

But what if the process reveals that the current Workflow isn't ideal? That there are some of those inefficiencies, bouncing between colours or swim lane roles?

The first step is identifying those issues, so well done! I'd encourage you to sit down (again, by yourself or with the team once you've got this documented) and agree which steps in this Workflow process are causing us the most pain.

Ask the question: where are we getting frustrated? You don't need to do a detailed analysis – the team will be able to tell you pretty quickly if there are difficult parts of the process, or steps that are really annoying.

You've now just identified the top priorities for reviewing and improving the performance of your operations! Maybe it's reworking your Workflow process.

Maybe it's finding other ways – like a checklist – to hold yourself accountable to following the Workflow process consistently. Maybe it's diving into those specific, frustrating steps to improve the policies or procedures that impact them.

The Start-Up Business Guide: 50 First Steps

Clear workflow processes work for your team and flow for your clients. They can also help remove all of those frustrations that may be bugging your team on a daily basis.

By Shan Naqvi & Jacob Aldridge

Key Relationships 1 of 3- Accountant

Chapter 18

"The first mistake I see a lot is the mistake of inexperience – most first time business owners make a lot of mistakes and run out of money before they listen to good, experience advisors."

"Understand the job of running a business (which includes leadership, marketing, sales, financial management, service, operations, product development, etc.) and surround yourself with great advisers and teammates who have the skills and experience you are lacking."

– Paul Hoyt

"The other main areas of the job that you're going to have to look at is you're going to have to deal with administration, which is a huge deficiency for most staff, so you have to go and learn what it is they're going to be doing. So, you need to go and do some sort of basic accounting course or spend time with your accountants.

"You need to write budgets, you need to understand what a chart of account is and how to write one, how to work with one. Each month, you need to sit down and look at your actual versus your budget so that you can understand where you're spending money, where you're making it, and where you're losing it.

"Absolutely I would do some things differently if I had my time again. The crazy arrogance was I thought "I know what I know," as opposed to today, it's like "I need to learn what I don't know." A lot of those things, when you say "What would I do differently?"

I would really get out there and learn the things I don't know – that funny, wonderful expression of "I would slide between the spreadsheets," and learn how to use those accounting software systems. I would have learned earlier how to read and write a chart of accounts. I would have done budgeting far earlier.

"Since that time, I've spent at least two hours a month with an accountant – and that's now over 12 years, a minimum of once a month – really learning the details of our business and understanding how in that area where I was so deficient, I can improve my capabilities.

I would say today that my understanding of how that back-end accounting side of our business works is a lot better than it certainly was at the start." – **Haesley Cush**

By Shan Naqvi & Jacob Aldridge

As *Paul Hoyt* notes, great businesses are not built by the business owner in isolation, but rather when you work together with a great group of experienced advisors.

Since we are both business coaches, you might think our advice would be that the first key relationship you need is a business coach! But this is absolutely *not* what we recommend – business coaching can bring a lot of value, but it usually takes time and in the first year of your business you need results fast.

Having a great business accountant will help you with this. They will be able to bring structure and financial recommendations that can be the difference between making a profit or running out of cash and having to close your business. Because they are working with dozens of other businesses just like yours, they can also bring specific, relevant business advice.

Many new business owners are worried about costs, and try to save money wherever they can. As a result, they either don't use an accountant or they try to use their personal accountant to do the business work. This makes them 'penny-wise and pound-foolish' – a good accountant will more than cover their own costs through their financial advice.

I remember starting my UK business and worrying about the £60/month my accountant was going to charge me ... in their first meeting they helped me structure my tax affairs in a way that saved me £3,000 every year in VAT payments. Do you think I ever thought of them as expensive again?

Don't be afraid to meet with multiple accountants, before choosing the one you want to work with. And make sure they are experienced working with start-up businesses of your size, and either in your industry or your product type.

I have seen many small businesses go to a Big 4 accounting firm thinking they must be better, only to be overcharged and treated poorly because those firms are built to service much larger organisations and as such don't have the skills to help small companies.

This step is easy: have you got an accountant you trust, that you can call to ask questions of, and who provides you with relevant business advice?

By Shan Naqvi & Jacob Aldridge

Key Relationship 2 of 3- Mentor

Chapter 19

Be sure to get someone on your team, at least as an advisor, who has been there and done it before – **Paul Hoyt**

What's the difference between a Mentor and a Coach? This can be difficult to answer, because many advisors in the marketplace use the two terms (as well as others like Trainer, Facilitator, Consultant, and Advisor) interchangeably.

Given the money and time you will invest in this relationship, understanding the answer and acting accordingly makes the difference between achieving a return on your investment and seeing those valuable resources wasted.

By definition, a Mentor is someone who has walked your path before. They usually have specific experience as a business owner in both your industry and your market. They can sit down with you and say 'Ah, when I was at your phase of the business I did these things to make a difference'.

As long as your industry hasn't changed all that much, then you've got great advice.

Coaching, in its purest form, is simply about asking you questions and drawing on your own knowledge. That can be helpful for embedding capability or giving you confidence in your own decisions, but it can't give you that additional perspective. A Coach asks questions … because they can't answer your questions!

So you can see how, in the earliest days of your start-up, a good Mentor is much more valuable.

"I made some big mistakes in the first couple of years of opening Harris, and probably primarily that was due to the extraordinary growth that we had in a short period of time. We went from 3 or 4 staff to 60 or 70 staff in about a 12-month period or something like that. As a result of that, that was very expensive.

I didn't have the right infrastructure, technology, systems, or the right people in the right roles. And so as a result of that, that got very expensive.

By Shan Naqvi & Jacob Aldridge

One of the key things looking back, what would I do differently this time around if I was starting a business, I would probably jump on a few more planes and go and speak with some other successful principals and look at "What are the fundamentals you need to have in place if you want to have a successful real estate business?" and have those firmly in place before you start." – **Phil Harris**

Like so many business owners, Phil Harris jumped in with his own expertise and didn't stop to think that he could learn from those who were already doing it. He built a successful business anyway, but it was fragile and dependent on him until he took the advice of his mentors and peers to make some simple changes.

The best thing about great Mentors is that they actually want to help, to give back. International business mentor and Coach Tom McCallum defines Mentoring as "an exchange of energy" – sometimes that can be money, but not always because the Mentor receives as much from the relationship as the person being Mentored.

So don't fear approaching the experts in your field and asking them to Mentor you. Use the magic word – "I'm starting my business and I would love your *help*" – and then arrange to meet. Be courteous. Be grateful. If you meet for lunch or over a coffee, make sure you pay. And ask the questions you need answers to.

A Mentoring relationship can be formal or informal. Maybe you meet a few times a year at a coffee shop; maybe you meet in their office on the second Tuesday morning of every month. Perhaps you might even have several Mentors, as long as their advice doesn't conflict or confuse you.

As long as they're receiving energy from the relationship, the relationship will continue to bring you value.

Do you already have a Mentor? If not, who would you like your Mentor to be? This week, reach out to introduce yourself and ask for help.

By Shan Naqvi & Jacob Aldridge

Context vs Content

Chapter 20

Every decision that you as a business owner make is powered by Context. What do we mean by that?

Context is the wider perspective that gives meaning to the Content, the Stuff that fills our daily lives. Context is Why we do what we do – why meaning "For what purpose?" not in a confrontational way.

I see a lot of great ideas in business fail because the owner – that's you – failed to give the team the right context in which to understand and implement their plan.

In a start-up business, that team includes everyone from your business and life partners through to your suppliers and your customers … and most importantly, it includes you and making sure that you are clear about why you are making the decisions that you make.

One of the realities of being a business owner is that the longer we're in business, the more team, the more clients, even the more money that we're bringing in, the more stuffed we get with that Content.

If however, you remain clear on why you're doing certain things and if your team are clear about why you're doing certain things then a whole lot of the issues that show up in the stuff will go away.

Let me give you a simple example that I actually see in a lot of partnerships: they sit down and decide that "Growth" is a priority. One of them goes and hires a new staff member. One of them goes and fires a staff member! And yet both think that that's the growth strategy.

For the first partner "Growth" meant more people, so we can service more clients and generate more revenue. The other partner saw that getting rid of some overhead would grow profit they were much more interested in the shorter term benefits of growing profit, which is also one way of defining "Growth".

So down in the Content, in the Stuff, they made very different decisions despite feeling aligned. And that was because they really didn't get to the heart of "Why?" Why do we want to grow? What do we actually mean by growth?

This is a decision that shows up in everything from big strategic elements to "who cleans the kitchen" and "who puts the paper back into the photocopier".

Speed v Quality

Here's another real business example, from a fence manufacturer I worked with. There were two clear teams in this business – the 3 guys in Sales and the 3 guys in the Factory who made the actual fences.

All of them wanted the business to succeed – they were 'on the same page'. But they brought a different context to their roles.

The Sales team ran a context of Speed – they knew clients wanted fast service and installation. The Factory team ran a context of Quality – they knew clients wanted the job done right and built to last.

Can you see the conflict here? When the Salesperson is under pressure to hit their targets, they were out overpromising clients about how fast it would happen; when the welder was making a decision, he was opting for quality – the client will understand if it takes an extra day, because the workmanship is so good. Constant clashes.

So who was right? Which is more important, speed or quality? There's no right or wrong answer.

That's the power of Context, and its trap. Because there's no one correct decision-making filter, you can create and lead your business however you choose.

But understand at all times that it's perfectly rational for your team members to be choosing their context, running their own filters – and it won't be obvious that they differ from yours.

What you want, need, is alignment. Because if you don't communicate to your team WHY you make the decisions you do, then chances are they will start making decisions for different reasons. And before too long, they'll be making different decisions to what you would do.

Right from the very start of your business journey, every time you make a key decisions ask yourself "Why did I choose that?" Better still, write those reasons down so you can remember and communicate them later, as you grow.

When communicating decisions or giving directions to your team, take the extra moment to communicate this reason why, the Context.

And when circumstances change, which they always do in the journey of a business, the time will come when you need to change a previous decision. (Maybe you have to raise prices, or restructure the team, or try a different marketing approach.)

When this happens, communicating the original Context, what has changed, and the new Context accelerates both your own decision-making and also the support of those around you.

Layers of Context

Chapter 21

Having talked about the difference between Content (What we do) and Context (Why we do it), we can now explore how all those different decisions in business combine together.

If you're like every other business owner, it doesn't take too much time for your head to be filled with all that content: so much stuff, so many competing ideas and opportunities, plus the never-ending to-do list. You're in need of a good flamethrower to clear things out.

Well that flamethrower is what I call the Layers of Context. When you apply this advanced Context framework, you can rapidly see how the key elements of your business either align or clash, and identify at any moment what your #1 priority in business needs to be.

You may be familiar with the approach, handed down from the large multinational business Toyota, called "The 5 Whys".

That approach suggests that for whatever the issue that shows up in the content of your business, if you ask "Why" five times you will eventually get to the very root cause of that problem.

The Layers of Context Framework detailed in this chapter gives "The 5 Whys" more structure, to make sure that those questions don't go off on a vast tangent.

Here's a list of the most common Contexts, or decision-making filters. From the top to the bottom, these act on each other.

Layer 1: VISION
- Personal Vision
- Cultural Vision
- Commercial Vision

Layer 2: STRATEGY
- Growth Plan
- Brand Promise
- Client Journey

Layer 3: RESOURCES
- Operational Structure

- Skills & Training
- Profit Formula

Layer 4: SYSTEMS
- Documented Systems & Processes

Layer 5: EXPECTATIONS
- Expectations Communicated & Managed

Most businesses try and fix problems from the bottom up, and sometimes to fix a problem you just need to reset Expectations. When you have the luxury to start a new organization however, you want to start making your decisions from the very top. If you can get clear from the top and work your way down then it's much easier.

The highest Layer of Context in your business is your Vision, This is the really big "why you decided to start this business".

The three key elements that sit at the Vision layer are your Personal Vision and Beliefs, the Cultural Vision you have for the company, and your Commercial goals, the dollars and cents objectives that you're looking to build. Each of these is detailed in other chapters in this essential guide.

By Shan Naqvi & Jacob Aldridge

If you have those Vision Contexts clear, it makes all your other decisions so much easier.

If you're clear on the Vision, you can then get clear on the Strategy you need for Layer 2. The three elements to the Strategy are your Growth Plan (what are the specific steps to take you from where you are now to where you want to go?), your Brand and Marketing Strategy (you need a presence in your marketplace, whether you're selling retail or B2B you need to be famous for something to help guide all of the elements that sit below), and the third element of Strategy is the Customer or Client Journey (this is a critical element for modern businesses because our customers have more choice than ever).

Mapping these elements at your Strategy level helps get you clear on the growth steps you need to move forward. Once you have a documented Vision and a clear Strategy, you then get into the Resources (Layer 3) within your business.

This is where a lot of the frustration can show up. The three elements to Resources are the Operational Structure that you have in place: do you have the right people doing the right job at the right time? Secondly, Skills and

Development: do your team have the right skills to execute their responsibilities?

The third element is your Profit Formula: revenue is vanity, profit is sanity, cash is reality and yet for a lot of new and growing businesses they really don't have the financial fundamentals at a Resource level to make sure that they're making money every month.

From here you start to get into some of the Content, some of the day-to-day elements that run your business. These are just as important because this is where your business actually happens, but they are less instructive in guiding your team.

Systems and Processes (Layer 4) don't need to be a mammoth effort unless you're scaling a mammoth business. However, I find a lot of businesses that 'just do things the way we've always done them' later discover losing one staff member can create havoc because that person was the only person who knew how to do certain things. They didn't have the critical Systems and Processes in place.

Lastly, one of the fundamental issues that shows up particularly if we're working from the bottom up is

Expectations (Layer 5). Are you and your team clear about all of the Expectations about who needs to do what? Are those expectations fully documented, and have they been communicated to the team?

If you've got a clear Vision and a Strategic roadmap to get you there, then you can structure the Resources appropriately and have them drive the Systems and Processes you need to set the right Expectations with every team member.

In this way, you make sure that the stuff is a whole lot easier.

So how do you rate yourself against all of those critical Contextual questions? A practical exercise you can run now and often is to score yourself against those 11 elements.

And use a really simple scoring system: just give yourself a TICK (we do this really well), CROSS (this is a problem keeping me awake sometimes), or NEUTRAL (we're not amazing but this works OK).

Use gut feel to make this exercise quick and simple. And don't try comparing your business against another, or against some imaginary, perfect organisation. Just compare how you feel with the current business versus the one you want to be building.

Success in business is not about having all those questions as TICKS. Because as you grow, things that used to work will break. That's normal, and why I recommend completing this exercise often.

Not sure where to focus your strategy time right now? The higher up on this framework that something has a CROSS, the more important it is. After all, there's no point improving your Profit Formula if your Commercial Vision isn't clear – you may be building a business that doesn't get you to where you want to go! And the same applies across all five layers.

Move up the different layers of context to get to the root cause, because solving the problem here will fix so many more issues in the stuff. You'll suddenly find that a business that had you 'stuffed' has you excited once again, or this start-up that was stalling and confusing once again has the clarity you desire.

By Shan Naqvi & Jacob Aldridge

Commercial Vision

Chapter 22

I wouldn't really call it a secret. I knew what I wanted, and so I went after it. I didn't hesitate to start, even though I had people telling me I was crazy ... I was scared and I didn't know what would happen when I launched, but I didn't let that stop me from just starting.

- **John Lee Dumas**

Peter Drucker taught us that **"Culture eats Strategy for Breakfast"**. Simon Sinek insisted that we must **"Start with why"** before we talk specifics. Dan Pink would lead us to believe that **"It's not about the money."**

You know who thinks it's not about the money? **People who already have money!**

There's a reason you're starting a business. Not a charity. Not just giving away your money or your expertise. You have created a commercial entity ... so don't ever feel bad for acknowledging that there's a commercial reality to your business and your life. (We don't claim Culture isn't important of course.)

The next chapter explores your Cultural Vision at depth, and we began this guide talking about your mindset and emotions well before we explored your business model. It's just that a business that doesn't make money doesn't last, and you can't achieve any of your cultural or lifestyle aims if your business no longer exists.)

So how clear are you about your Commercial Vision? Have you shared this with someone – your spouse or partner where applicable, your business partner where applicable, or at least your accountant and mentor?

Your Commercial Vision has 4 Corners: Business Income, Personal Income, Business Equity, and Personal Wealth.

Personal Income is what you pay yourself. At start-up, the question is "What do I **Need** to earn?" because your income has to cover bare essentials like rent, food, school fees etc. If you have savings or a supportive spouse such that you don't *need* to earn anything, that's fantastic because it means total re-investment into your business.

You also want to ask "What do I **Want** to earn?" Don't be flippant with this question – we'd all love to earn $50 million a year for doing very little. What's the personal income that would actually fund the life you want to live?

This is a helpful number to know, because knowing it helps you focus on getting there ... and also stops you from blowing past it, paying yourself more and more each year at the expense of reinvesting in the sustainability of your golden goose business.

Business Income is what Net Profit you want to achieve (plus your Income if you pay yourself regularly).

While you want to ask yourself the Personal Income questions first, the Business Income is the first of the 4 Corners you have to master. Build the cash flow and profit margins so you have the funds to convert into Personal Income, and through reinvestment into Business Equity.

Again, don't fall for ego and pick a large and mysteriously round number. What's the spare cash flow you want coming out of the business at this time that will make a difference?

Business Equity is linked to your Business Valuation. The great thing is that income follows assets, so the more you are building your valuation the more you are creating a platform for future income.

Do you know how business valuations are calculated in your industry and region? While common practices vary, these are usually measured as a Multiple of either Income or Net Profit. The higher the Multiple, the more confident the value or buyer feels your business will continue to deliver its current (or higher) income or profit.

(This is sometimes inversed as a cap rate risk percentage, but it's the same simple concept. I won't pay a dime for your business if I think it will go broke without you tomorrow; Amazon and Apple are worth $100 Billion because they have the systems, talent, channels, brand, and proven scale in place to suggest they would continue profitably for decades even if they switched off business model innovation today.)

Personal Wealth is the Net Worth you seek for your family. Ultimately, your start-up business is not your real business – your real business is the asset base owned by your family (of which your Business Equity is one, likely important, component).

'Financial Independence' is having a Personal Wealth that can fund your Personal Income ambitions. This is often calculated by multiplying your Personal Income Want number by 25 – the so-called "4% Rule" because that volume of funds invested can pay you out 4% of the starting principle, adjusted for inflation, and rarely run out of money. If this topic is of interest, we recommend searching for more detailed explanations online.

As a simple example:

- If your Personal Income want is $100,000 per annum
- Then your Personal Wealth vision might be $2.5 million ($100,000 x 25)

You might want your Business Income to be $200,000 (this would pay you $100,000 each year, while your Wealth was still growing, and have another $100,000 to reinvest in the business)

And your goal might be a Business Equity valuation of $600,000 (which is Net Profit times a Multiple of 3; and would mean you need $1.9 million of your Personal Wealth to be in other assets like real estate or stocks).

So how clear are you about your Commercial Vision? Do you have a number in each of those four corners? Now go and share this with someone!

Cultural Vision

Chapter 23

How I define success is that it's essential for it to be your own version of success, not the version of success handed to you by society, friends, parents, classmates, co-workers, colleagues, and acquaintances.

Actually take the time to sit down and define your own version of success. Success is not necessarily about fame, money, or power – it's about being true to yourself no matter what, living your values, being an example for others, helping others when you can, and being authentic.

When you are living an authentic life on your own terms, you are more successful than you may have initially realized. – **Jeff Davis**

OK, here are the two dumbest things I hear all the time about Culture:
 1) It's organic – you can't control it, and
 2) I think we have a great culture

How long would your business last if you told the tax department the same story you tell about Culture?

"Oh, Profits man, you can't control those. But we're doing pretty well financially, I think."

Let me be honest – if you're not in charge of your Culture, then your culture is out of control and probably one of the reasons why great ideas aren't working in your business.

It doesn't have to be this way.

From the very day you start your business, you have a Culture. Now, if it's just you, or just you and your business partners, you don't have to do anything to define that culture – it's a reflection of you, and because the business is so small you control how the business feels every day.

Once you start recruiting people, chances are you will make instinctive cultural decisions. You'll be hiring people you liked, who were like you, and this ensures that the culture is steady.

The risk comes in a few years, or sooner if you're a fast-growth start-up. You're not as hands-on anymore. You may not talk to everyone, every day. You may not even be involved in some of the recruitment choices anymore. And so the Culture you think is occurring may not be.

Most business owners in this situation go looking for the big culture rocks – Friday afternoon drinks, Christmas parties, birthday cakes. That's nice and all, but if I hate coming to work every day then no amount of banoffee pie on my birthday is going to make me want to stay, let along be super productive.

A Culture System

Now, just having a moan about the good, bad and ugly won't change much. If you want to build a great culture for the long term, you need a culture system. Here's the one I build with my clients.

It's all about defining:

- WHO your ideal team member is
- WHY you are in business – what's your mission or purpose?

WHAT are your key values – these 3-5 values are critical Contexts, like we talked about in *Chapter 19*.

How will you implement these ideals – because a Mission Statement and Values on a wall that aren't supported by agreed behaviours and unique rituals can be even worse than not doing this exercise at all.

This can be done in an afternoon ... or it may take several sessions or a Culture project team. As the business leader, you need to be involved and approve the final decisions, but don't think you can do this on your own. Involve the team – after all, it's their culture too.

Lastly, this can be done too soon. Your primary focus as a start-up business is to generate revenue. Culture will help you do that, especially as you build a team, but it's not going to have the same effect as Sales Training or Product Development.

In the early days when you are still controlling the Culture of a small business, sometimes it pays to be mindful of how the team are feeling ... without committing to a full blown Culture project.

After all, there are plenty of great start-ups with legendary cultures ... who shut down fast when the money runs out. In business, the only way to live your culture every day is to also be profitable.

Risk Profile

Chapter 24

Being an entrepreneur is awesome. You are able to be your own boss and answer to yourself. It also allows you to define your own version of success. While working as an entrepreneur often takes longer hours than a normal 9-to-5 job, it can be more enjoyable and rewarding.

Knowing that your products and services are truly helping someone else is one of the best feelings in the world. **– Jeff Davis**

Understanding your Business Risk Profile is a critical topic for anyone who's in business – as well as their business and life partners, and even the leadership team. Your Risk Appetite is an important context for the decisions you make, especially when significant investments of time or money are involved.

You may be familiar with Risk Profiles from a financial planning perspective: at a very low risk, 1 out of 10, you might put your money in the bank or under a mattress; at a 10 out of 10 high risk you might go and invest in a warzone territory because that's a real up-and-coming economy!

In business, it's a very similar concept where some individuals are low risk, others are naturally just a higher risk, and this is then reflected in their behaviours.

The challenge that comes with this is that we as entrepreneurs are naturally more of a high risk than the population at large, which also means most of our team are going to have a lower risk than we do.

When we make strategic decisions and communicate them, the team can feel disconnected or even fearful of a decision they feel is a higher risk than necessary.

But taking risks is a critical part of starting a business. Without taking risks we can never innovate, seize an uncertain opportunity, or even invest our time in a venture where there is no guarantee of success.

Yet without awareness of a Business Risk tool, entrepreneurs struggle to explain that we're taking risks in this business and that's why we're in business! As a result, you can find that the team have resistance to your ideas.

In partnerships you have multiple directors in a business, so the issue of Risk can show up when different partners have different risk profiles and everyone is trying to have a conversation about what the business needs.

Someone with a high-risk profile in a partnership may feel that the others are holding them back, are short-sighted, or are frustrating their aspiration.

The partner with the lowest risk profile in the group may feel that the others gambling the future of the business, moving too fast, and not thinking their ideas through.

In these situations it's not about right or wrong – it's just about understanding those different preferences, and ideally setting the risk profile for the overall business.

The third and final application of Business Risk creates a lot of challenge in start-up businesses is when the spouse of the owner (whether they're working in the business or not) has a much lower business risk profile than the one who's gone out and started the business.

This can create a massive amount of tension when it feels like business decisions are pulling the relationship apart, over and above the natural overwhelm and anxiousness of a start-up. In these situations it's a similar conversation to the multiple directors: making an agreement between the two of you as to where the business needs to be.

On the scale of 1 to 10, I've not yet met a successful business owner who had a risk profile of less than 6. Business is about taking risks and seeing how they work out.

Risk doesn't mean 'Risky', and there are ways to mitigate the risks that you may be taking. You can't avoid taking risks if you want your business to grow.

Are you clear about your Risk Appetite, as a number between 1 and 10? What about your life or business partners? Are there wide differences, or not? And if there are some big differences – how do you choose a middle-ground number for the business overall so that the business can take the risks it needs to grow.

4 Critical Partnership Questions - Strategic

Chapter 25

There are many reasons why businesses with multiple founders work better than solopreneurs ... and there are also many people in successful businesses who will tell you to never to take on a partner.

So how do you know if having a business partner is right for you? More importantly, how do you know if this person (or group) is the right person to partner with?

In this chapter, we will explore the 4 Key Strategic Questions that you have to ask yourself and any potential business partner. If you aren't aligned at a strategic level, then the partnership is doomed to failure.

Similarly, if you have clarity of things like your Commercial and Cultural Vision and confidence that you can achieve this on your own, then you have to ask: what value is a business partner?

A great partner will make the business journey more enjoyable, help you share the responsibilities and burden of business ownership, and either help you achieve greater commercial success or the same success sooner.

Those are reasons for having a business partner: loyalty, sympathy, and fear are terrible reasons for sharing equity.

⟩ *Partnership Question 1. What is the Commercial Vision for this enterprise?*

How big do you want to grow (revenue, staff numbers)?
Is this an Income or an Equity business?

It's not essential that both partners have an identical vision, but they must be aligned. If you want to reach $24 million in revenue in 5 years and your partner wants $3 million, then you have a fundamental issue.

Your desire to recruit, train, handover, grow will overcome their unwillingness to do so, no matter how 'great' or 'easy' you think it will become.

An analogy I use is two parties planning an overseas holiday. To get there, you have to walk down the garden path, take a taxi to the airport, and hop on a plane to your destination.

If you want to go to Bora Bora, and your partner does not, it's important to know where they want to go. Sometimes, their vision only extends to the end of the garden path, or to the airport.

The taxi trip alone is their dream holiday, and they don't mind farewelling you (i.e., handing over equity or control of the business) so you can fly to Bora Bora. Your visions are aligned and this trip can take you both where you want to go.

But if they want to fly to London, or take a cruise, or never leave the living room, then you have a problem.

The two fundamental elements of your Commercial Vision are size and purpose. Specifically, how big (or not) do you want to be? And is this primarily an Income or an Equity opportunity?

Each of these choices will impact daily or weekly decisions you have to make in your business, so misalignment here will mean your partnership will become a tug-of-war not a successful venture.

By Shan Naqvi & Jacob Aldridge

> *Partnership Question 2. What are the Cultural Values we choose for this enterprise?*

Would I bring this person home for dinner?
What is our aligned Intent? What are the 3-5 core values of our venture?

It's surprising how many business owners go into business with people they don't like, because the commercial opportunity is so great. It's less surprising how many of these ventures fail (most of them!).

The simplest way to align Culture is to genuinely assess whether you want to be in business with the other person. The barbecue test – would I bring this person home for a family meal? – is one I follow.

Those seeking a more comprehensive answer may decide to complete the Cultural Vision exercise from Chapter 22. Can you agree on your Who, Why, and What (3-5 Core Values)?

Don't give in to temptation and have a long list of values. This is about determining whether you are compatible – if you can't work together to define a shortlist of core values, you will struggle to implement an aligned Culture as the venture grows.

⟩ *Partnership Question 3. Are your natural Behavioural preferences complementary?*

What are your Communication styles? What are your Risk appetites?
What are your Leadership strengths? What are your natural Pace tendencies?

It's easy when forming a partnership to focus on the greatness of the opportunity. But ensuring your natural behavioural preferences will work together is a crucial part of Cultural Due Diligence.

Every investor who has seen ideal Commercial Due Diligence descend into failure recognises the role partners and leaders have in a venture's success ... or otherwise.

I recommend comparing and contrasting these four behaviours in a Partnership because they cover aspects where alignment is key (Communication, Risk) and others where a balance is preferable (Leadership, Pace), while at all times acknowledging that we are all a composite of many different traits.

Case Study – Drew and Yvette

Drew had successfully grown her style consultancy into a million dollar business, and brought Yvette on board to help franchise the system for national growth. Yvette's package was a mix of income (below market rate) and equity (to compensate, and align their incentives).

Having completed Commercial Due Diligence, the partnership was formed, but they agreed that no equity would change hands for the first 6 months, while they undertook Cultural Due Diligence. They had identified potential areas of conflict to monitor.

During this time it became clear that Drew and Yvette's Risk and Pace profiles were incompatible. Drew was a risk taker who moved fast, and was used to being the sole CEO making decisions.

Yvette was entrepreneurial, but more methodical – this was a complementary skill set, but meant partnership meetings were constantly frustrating with Drew feeling handcuffed and Yvette feeling she never had a say before decisions were made.

After six months it was agreed not to proceed with the partnership. A messy business divorce was avoided and by identifying that it was behaviours, not personalities that were the problem their relationship was able to continue.

> ***Partnership Question 4. Who has which preferences regarding Income, Equity, and Control?***

What is the order of your preferences?
What is the order of your partner's?

A fundamental error most new partnerships make is viewing Income, Equity, and Control (IEC) as the same decision. For example, they give an equal share of equity, pay all partners the same salary, and have equal say over decisions. This needn't be the case.

If you had to select one of these three as being of primary importance to you, which would it be – Income, Equity, or Control? Which is least important? You now have your priorities.

Compare these with your partner's. If they match, this has potential benefits for your commercial vision but may create conflicts in how you structure the business.

In particular, if both of you want Control you may create the molasses of decision-making-by-consensus. If neither of you want Control, who will step up to make the big decisions?

Some common solutions that acknowledge different priorities include:
- Creating joint ventures rather than simple partnerships, to incentivise an equity-minded individual;
- Incorporating Control features into the Shareholders Agreement or Constitution. For example, specifying which decisions the CEO can make will empower that individual. Specifying decisions that require a super-majority (2/3rd or 3/4tr majority) of the Board or Shareholders (taking on debt, new partners, expenses over $10,000 etc.) ensures minority shareholders still retain some control;

- Different Share Classes can also be used to de-link equity percentages from control, with the Murdoch Family and Mark Zuckerberg being pertinent examples of where equity has been sold without control being given away.

Even when forming your new partnership, it's worth noting that Structures may change over time as your IEC preferences change.

For example, they may be revised to support younger partners wanting accelerated growth AND older partners adding value while winding down, rather than the traditional professional services model of expecting all partners to act similarly – which restricts young go-getters (who then leave) and demands the wrong focus from knowledgeable senior partners who don't want to be pushed (and then leave).

Are you asking all the right questions?

Your answers about Vision (how big!), Behaviours (how fast!), and IEC will help as we shift into the Operational space in the next chapter, where the questions to ask become more specific.

By Shan Naqvi & Jacob Aldridge

4 Critical Partnership Questions - Operational

Chapter 26

In the last chapter we asked the 4 strategic questions potential business partners need to ask each other. As promised, there are also 4 operational questions. And many a great idea in business has failed because some of these expectations weren't set right from the beginning.

If you have a great idea - for a new, or your existing business - and a potential partner lined up, asking and debating these questions can feel unproductive.

Trust me when I tell you - it's better to have a partnership fall over because you couldn't answer these questions, than to discover your incompatibility at a crucial and expensive juncture down the road.

Partnership Question 5. What are the expected upfront Contributions?
- o Contribution of money
- o Contribution of time
- o Contribution of clients / leads
- o Other

When starting the new venture, who will be contributing what (in terms of money, time, clients, and other elements such as office space, equipment, intellectual property, or networks) during the Start-Up phase?

If you don't have a simple business plan, you may need to draft one in order to answer this question. It needn't be detailed – but all parties will want to know whether you'll need $1,000 or $100,000 invested before the business becomes self-sustaining.

Note particularly that dollars aren't the only factor when determining value contributed, a mistake that can cause frustration now or in the future when the equity splits are reviewed.

Partnership Question 6. What are the expected Contributions over time?

Covering the same elements, what is each party expected to contribute in the future?

This may be necessary contributions (e.g., $5,000/Month for payroll rather than $50,000 upfront) or they may be linked to milestones, desired and feared. For example, success in one location (however defined) may trigger an additional investment from the partners to open a new location.

Alternatively, what happens if the business fails to become profitable / self-sustaining before the money runs out? Are partners expected to invest more, or will this be optional (with the possible consequence of diluting equity stakes for those who do not contribute more)?

As you could imagine, many good businesses have failed to fully launch because they ran out of money while the partners argued over who would keep it afloat.

Partnership Question 7. What are the expectations for Salaries and Dividends?
- o   What does each partner need?
- o   What does each partner want?

Money is energy. And that applies to business partners as much as the business itself. It's not a good idea to assume or decide that all partners are paid the same salary. Indeed, this is part of the common mistake of equating Income, Equity and Control – "if we're both partners, we should both earn the same amount".

Incomes work best when they reflect the specific contribution of each partner to the business and pay them market rates. Take senior and junior technicians, for example – if they are partners paid the same salary, then either one is underpaid, or one is overpaid. Neither result is energising.

But in business negotiations, especially involving a start-up venture that may not be able to pay market rates, the salary conversation can be difficult. Nobody wants to be greedy; nor do they want to be taken advantage of.

The first question to ask then is 'What do you need to earn?' In other words, what do you need to be taking home to your family so that money isn't a major stress? This may not be market rate, and the shortfall is part of your investment in the company (either specifically through the Shareholders agreement, or just energetically).

Don't create a situation where one of the partners needs to do work on the side to pay the school fees. You'll also need to trust each other's responses, especially if they vary wildly – trust, after all, is critical to a partnership.

The second question is 'What do you want to earn?' This can be a massive number, by which point it usually includes dividends (share of company profits) as well as Salary. It will inform the Commercial Vision (if you want to earn $500,000pa but only build a $500,000 company, you have a problem) and also allow you to set some milestones for partner pay rises as the business grows.

In this way, nobody feels stressed from day one, and all partners know that their income will grow with the business.

Note that Shareholders who only contribute capital are generally not rewarded with a Salary. Their cash returns come from Dividends, which are linked to Equity.

Partnership Question 8. Who has what Functional Responsibilities?

In a one person business, this is easy. Who sets the vision, defines the culture, negotiates contracts, delivers great customer service, and cleans the kitchen each night? You do!

But in a partnership, whether a two-person venture or overseeing a growing enterprise, these specific responsibilities need to be defined. The alternative is inefficiencies, with both partners giving conflicting instructions to staff while neither of you remember to process payroll.

At a top level for operational responsibilities, you can use tools like the Layers of Context from Chapter 21 or the four RNR Colours in Chapter 16. You want a meaningful list of all the areas in your business – nothing too long, but long enough to separate out the essentials as they apply in your business right now.

Only one person can be responsible for each area. And it may not even be a partner. Responsibility does not mean having to do all of it, however – tasks can be delegated.

This may mean Partner A reports to Partner B when it comes to Sales, but the roles are reversed when it comes to Culture. A one-page Responsibility Chart, at least, makes these responsibilities clear BEFORE you get into business together.

By Shan Naqvi & Jacob Aldridge

Key Financial Metrics

Chapter 27

In a discussion, **Shan** asked **Andrew Vorster** how a start-up business owner could efficiently reach $1 million in revenue.

"They can either focus on building one big thing that they can sell for $1 million OR they can focus on one small thing that they can sell for $1 to 1 million people. So that's not helpful, but my point is to demonstrate the futility of focussing on $1 million revenue - who cares about revenue anyway?

"The focus should be on profit - if the business owner was to get $1 million in revenue at a 5% net profit margin, they have made $50,000 - but if I get $500,000 in revenue at 15% net profit margin then I have made $75,000. So I would say to the business owner who asks me a question like that "you're asking me the wrong question." – **Andrew Vorster**

Wouldn't it be great if before you started a business the government put you through an accelerated MBA – taught you all that stuff you need to know about managing a team and understanding your financials?

OH HELL NO – ain't nobody got time for that!

And so we find ourselves as business owners with a strong gut feel for how the business is doing, but not necessarily a strong grasp on our financials.

> **There's too much month at the end of the money.**
> **We feel great, until a large, irregular bill falls due.**
> **Our Accountant tells us we made a great profit last month, but there's nothing in the bank account and now we have a tax bill.**

Sometimes great ideas and even great business fail for a simple lack of money.

The basics of your business financials are simple:
- Sell your Product - Revenue
- Pay your Costs – Variable and Fixed
- Make a Profit – Operational, Net, or EBITDA
- Turn it into Cash – Cash at Bank
- Spend it wisely – Make Mindful Choices

By Shan Naqvi & Jacob Aldridge

You would be surprised to see how many businesses don't give sufficient attention to the bottom line Profit – ensuring that revenue exceeds expenses.

Of course, your bottom line is the just start – once you make a profit, you need to turn it into cash. You won't be able to invest, or pay your team, if clients are taking 60 or 90 days to pay your invoices.

And then once you have that cash, spend it wisely. You can be as detailed with a budget as you like (so, not at all then?) as long as you avoid the cycle of spending money when you have it, and worrying when you don't.

Don't let the ego of Revenue drive your decision-making. Revenue without Profit is only sustainable with very deep pockets.

Don't let 'your bottom line' sting your great ideas in the backside. Focusing on Profit can mean not making investments when you need to, or not being careful with Cash Flow *(Chapter 30)*.

Your financial numbers tell a story. Too many business owners just can't read the language. Too much growth is as fatal as too little. Reading your financial reports at least monthly – and understanding them – will empower your daily decision-making.

Don't do this alone. Ask your Accountant for at least Quarterly Management Reports, and a discussion about what they mean for you.

And don't forget your personal finances *(Chapter 27)*. Your business is just one part of your Personal Vision. Don't make it profitable and valuable, only to have that slip away through your personal finances.

By Shan Naqvi & Jacob Aldridge

Personal vs Business Finances

Chapter 28

We've talked about your commercial Structures and some of your Key Financial Metrics. Now let's get practical and talk about your bank accounts and your personal budget – because these minor administrative decisions can have a major impact on whether your business survives its first year.

Bank Accounts

'Best Practice' banking that we recommend is having at least 3 separate bank accounts:

- Your business trading or general account
- Your personal bank account
- A business saving or tax account

At the beginning, especially if the best structure for you right now is as a sole trader under your own name, it's common to just have clients paying money (and you paying expenses) directly using your personal bank account. This gets messy real quick, especially if you don't have strict personal budget systems.

Three clients paid this week – feeling rich, let's all go out to dinner! Oh crap, I have tax due next week plus a big inventory order so I can win the big new client.

Much ... and we can't stress this enough, **MUCH** easier to set up a separate bank account for your business (even if it's in your own name still). Come tax time, this will save you hours of sifting personal from business, and it will prevent you from celebrating with your money too early.

The second business account is helpful for those longer term expenses, in particular ensuring that you are putting money aside for the inevitable tax obligations (Congratulations!) and/or any future investments you want to make in equipment, premises, staff etc.

Ring-fencing this money again makes it easier not to feel your financial situation is healthier than it truly is, and spending money that's ultimately isn't really yours to spend.

Personal Budget

How strict you need to be with multiple bank accounts does depend how systemised your Personal Budget is. If you are (like most people) naturally inclined to spend first and save whatever is left without regard to a personal budget, then you will be a financial liability to your business.

It's one thing in life to have "too much month at the end of the money", because you can live on noodles for a week; when running out of cash means missing payroll, ruining a relationship with a key supplier, or skipping a taxation obligation then the consequences are much worse.

And the most common way businesses miss those obligations is the business owner treating the business bank account as their own personal bank account, and then spending too much of it on things that didn't deliver a timely ROI to the business (like, um, Uber Eats).

Set yourself a simple personal budget, based on the personal income you Need (not Want, not yet) to cover the essentials. Now, 'essentials' doesn't mean living on bread and water – man cannot live on bread alone, so have some flexibility.

If you've never set a personal budget before, there are two approaches:

Get detailed by tracking all of your actual expenses for a period. Define some categories, determine how much you need for each category per annum, and divide by 12 for monthly 'mini accounts'.

Make sure your personal income funds every mini account, and start distributing money into them each payday. Some mini accounts (like Groceries) may be spent every pay cycle; others (like home maintenance) may build up to large amounts over time. Apps that integrate with your bank account often do some of this automatically.

Have an 'Unbudget'. Estimate what you need to pay yourself each month. Allocate 70% for essential bills, 10% for savings, and 20% for fun. See how you go managing this budget for a few months, and tweak the variables (income, and those percentages) accordingly.

Having good financial habits in your personal life is a helpful foundation for your business. You'll note that we haven't suggested a Business Budget anywhere in this Guide – that's because, as a start-up, your Budget is likely to be imaginary and woefully inaccurate, making it a complete waste of time.

By Shan Naqvi & Jacob Aldridge

In Year 2, when you have some real financial data and experience to build upon, creating a Business Budget can be more meaningful – especially when you have a team to share financial responsibility with.

How are your personal financial habits? What can you do practically with your business finances to protect both business and personal monies?

Making Investment Decisions

Chapter 29

Being an entrepreneur and working at a job do not have to be mutually exclusive. The best time to start a business is when you have stable income from a job. The entrepreneurial life is often glorified, but the truth is that it takes money to earn money.

It's very helpful to have income and savings to support you while you go through the ups and downs of the entrepreneurial life. I don't agree with the saying, "Jump off the cliff and grow wings on the way down." It's important to be practical.

I suggest not leaving your job until you've replaced that income with your entrepreneurial endeavours, or at the very least have seen some growth and income come in from your business.

Also, you can start to think like an entrepreneur while at your job. Creativity and innovation will not only help you to succeed as an entrepreneur, but in all areas of your life."
– Jeff Davis

By Shan Naqvi & Jacob Aldridge

Every penny you spend in business needs to be deliberate. This is especially the case when you have no other source of income (we like *Jeff Davis's* practical advice above, while also believing that many times your business won't work until you take the risk to dive in completely).

This also continues to be the case when you achieve some level of success – don't let the fact you have money mean you respect it less.

Both of us value generosity, and we believe an abundance mindset helps grow our businesses. But as **Shan** learned, being too generous can backfire.

Early in my career, I was a very simple man with very little knowledge, some experience, and connections with some of the world's finest business consultants. I was totally depressed because I didn't know how to make a living.

I picked up my phone one night when my need for money had reached a critical threshold. I called an American business coach I knew, and when he said "Hey Shan, what's up?" I knew I needed to be honest. I was so unhappy. So, with a very low voice, I said, "I'm not all right." And our conversation started.

That generosity of time and wisdom was what I needed. He gave me some things to do, and I started to make some money. It was very little, but it was something and it was a helpful amount for where I live in Pakistan. How little? I had one income stream making $60 a month, and I was very happy with that.

From that amount, my work began to grow. I finally started to make some good money and my life was changed. My thoughts changed with the money.

There was a ghost of Charity on my head. I had been helped, and now I was in a financial position to help other people. When I did so, it made me feel good. Paying more and more people became my addiction. Spending money all over the place became my ideal thing to do.

My life became really complicated. The first people I helped were asking for help, and then they started taking cash as their wages. They were never worried-and they knew that I was always there to help them. I was called as an angel in public. But in reality, I was just a kind person. Just a people-pleaser!

By Shan Naqvi & Jacob Aldridge

I used to curse myself after giving people my hard-earned money. Especially when I didn't have any more money left.

A person who was content with $1 USD was not satisfied with me paying them, or giving them, more. I became a person who couldn't pay for his own life, yet I was paying a lot of other peoples' expenses.

These days were more complicated than the early days when I had no money. I was so tense. So worried about it. Well, so depressed.

Going through the internet, I read hundreds of articles about finding some help for these financial habits. But really, nothing helped me.

Every financial advisor said like **STOP GIVING PEOPLE MONEY**; and it never helped. Sometimes willpower can't play a role on its own. You've got to go deeper and deeper to figure out the actual solutions.

Now, searching here and there, I've discovered something that's changed my entire life. And these steps apply to every investment you make in business – whether that's people (staff, suppliers), equipment, materials, marketing and so on.

Here's how improve your financial habits (and stop paying people you don't owe):

1) **Write down on a piece of paper what happens if you don't pay that person.**

I'm not talking about not paying people you owe money to, your Creditors. This is making future payments, future commitments. What happens when you refuse to pay someone anymore?

I found my answer wasn't about the commercial reality of my business – I didn't write down how much the business would struggle without those investments. Instead, I had thoughts like "I would be a bad person", "I would be responsible if something bad happened to them because they didn't have my money".

The idea is to touch upon your core beliefs, to find out what's going on in your head, and actually change those core beliefs. For me, I had to learn that it is not my responsibility to pay others. They may have reasons for needing money, and I may empathise with them.

They may have a great skillset or product that could help a businessman like me. But if it wasn't actually helping me, if I didn't need that skillset right now? Then I had to take responsibility for my life, my money, and my business.

Trust me, many people are fake. You're a business owner, and you've got to save money to grow your business. And a lot of other feelings to stop the addiction.

2) *Figure out why you should not pay them.*

Everyone will have reasons why you should pay them. They have the best software, the best marketing knowledge, they have helped other businesses and so on.

You have to find the reason why you should not pay them! The easiest way is to actually know your financial situation. Do you actually have any spare money? Do you have enough money for your needs?

If you can't afford an investment – and it's a great investment – then it's OK to ask "How can I pay for this?" But if it's not a good investment, and you don't have the money, that's a good enough reason no to pay someone.

Even when you have lots of money, though, you have to use that money to keep growing your business. Many start-ups stay small because the owner begins paying themselves too much, too soon, or being too generous with their money in other ways.

3) *Whenever someone asks you to give them money, do this.*

First, have a money buddy. (This may be another friend, especially if they are a business owner too. It may be your accountant or mentor!) When someone asks you for money or tries to sell you something, send your money buddy a message (email, text or phone call, or meet in person).

Just let somebody know that someone is asking you for money. They may not even reply. Just having someone to listen can help keep you accountable to yourself.

Then don't make a quick decision to spend money. (It's OK to make quick decisions not to spend money.) Take a while, at least 24-48 hours so that you can think deeply about the decision. It is always important to take time before making a commitment. If I spend this money, what benefit will I receive in return?

By Shan Naqvi & Jacob Aldridge

This return on investment needs to have a meaningful impact on your business or your life. Usually, this means a financial return (if I spend $5,000 on this website, will it bring me $20,000 in more sales quickly?) or a return on time and energy (if I catch a taxi instead of public transport, what can I do with the extra 30 minutes in my office?).

Spending money because it's easier, when it doesn't have a return, is not wise.

The thing is, there are a lot of start-up entrepreneurs who make good money, but making money is not the key. The real key is to learn to save enough to expand. It doesn't matter how much you do before you save your pennies.

You may be living a paycheck-to-paycheck like millions of people, and that will potentially hold you back from success and become a true entrepreneur.

You can support people in a lot of other ways, and money is not the only one. Why don't you instruct them on how to make a little money?

Trust me, this is the real help. Not being the one who gives them the money, especially if you don't have the money.

By Shan Naqvi & Jacob Aldridge

Cash Flow

Chapter 30

According to the same CB Insights analysis, "running out of cash" is the second most common reason for start-up failure – in other words, it's possible to have a great product-market fit, an excellent business model, and a sustainable sales system ... and then fail in business because you were too successful, and the cash you needed to survive disappeared.

"Most founders of early stage start-ups that I meet can't tell me when they will bill their first dollar. If they don't know when they will start to generate revenue then how do they know how much cash they need to breakeven, let alone profitability?

"Even well-funded start-ups (I mean multi-million dollars in funding) have frequently failed by running out of cash before they reach profitability because they tried to scale too quickly and didn't fully appreciate the impact this would have on cash flow.

> " Cash is the life blood of any enterprise - stay on top of it" – **Andrew Vorster**

Revenue is Vanity, Profit is Sanity, and Cash is King. Yet Cash Flow can be confusing, and beyond the numbers has an emotional impact on you and your team. As they begin generating revenue, most business owners become confused when the 'Profit' on their financial statements seems worlds apart from the cash in their bank account.

This is perfectly normal (especially for businesses with mid-to-low gross profit margins, since inventory or staff are often paid well in advance of the customers paying their bills).

In this chapter we will explore how staff, owners, and your accountant all view your revenue and expenses differently - and why that creates stress.

Plus how you can implement some process and mindset changes with your team to put cash back in the bank for investing back into growing your business.

We discussed some financial terms in Chapter 15 about understanding your Break Even Point. (That's the point where your revenue covers all your expenses each month, above which you are making a profit.)

As you grow, however, you will notice that your cash doesn't always keep up with your profit margins, so we need to discuss some additional financial concepts.

These are the key elements of your operating cash flow, in terms of numbers AND in terms of the emotional impact they have on you as a business and as a business owner.

1) *Revenue*

Revenue is the top line (i.e., the top of your Profit & Loss Statement) money coming in.

In some businesses, with 'accrual' accounting, Revenue is measured when Invoices are sent – the Revenue is "accrued" even if it has yet to be received.

Not all start-up businesses operate that way, and for the purposes of tracking your Cash Flow you need to use a "Cash" accounting method.

This means, for the purposes of your operating cash flow, Revenue is the money you actually receive.

2) *Variable Costs / Cost of Sales / Cost of Goods Sold (COGS)*

We won't bore you with technical accounting terms, so we're going to lump all these slightly-different terms into one definition. Variable Costs are expenses that you will only incur when you sell your product or service. For example:

- A commission you have to pay to a salesperson or distributor
- Bank fees on the customer's credit card
- The cost of buying the product you just sold (We'll come back to this one later).

For the purposes of visualising your Cash Flow, think of Revenue as all the money coming in this month; then think of Variable Costs as the first amount of money that comes out. Your P&L Statement is probably set up to reflect this sequence as well.

First Emotional Cash Flow Drama! One of the challenges you will have as a business owner is that your team will usually have a pretty good idea of your Cost of Sales, but nothing below that.

This means that when they think about how profitable your business is they think about the Revenue and they think only about the impact of the Variable Costs: they think the rest of your Revenue is all profit! Of course, you know better.

You're well aware that the next thing sitting there is expenses all of those other overheads that are not related specifically to getting sales out the door.

3) Fixed Costs

Fixed Costs are the expenses you have to pay every month no matter what. Things like your rent, most of your staff, a lot of overheads, leases, software and so on. We explored this in more detail in *Chapter 15*.

As a start-up business, you want to be minimising the size of your Fixed Costs, especially ongoing commitments like leases. Sadly, we've seen business that have failed fast (which can be a good thing) ruin the business owner's life because the owner still had to pay office and equipment leases for years after the business had closed.

Of course, you also need to take risks in business and invest where you see a return. It's not about 'not spending any money', just about being careful to spend it wisely because these Fixed Costs will carry on every month.

Your staff will often be oblivious to the size of these overheads. I remember during the last Recession, one client sharing the monthly office Rent with their team.

It equated to about $10,000 per person per year (so it wasn't even a flashy office) – staff earning $60,000 per year were amazed at all the extra costs associated with employing them, and that was even before things like computers and training were paid for!

4) Operating Profit / Net Profit

By common accounting standards, Revenue minus Variable Costs minus Fixed Costs equals Operating Profit. This is where some business owners can get confused by Cash Flow. Just like the team finish this exercise early (by only thinking about Revenue and Variable Costs), many business owners finish early by thinking Operating Profit will equal the cash in the bank account.

In some businesses, the numbers will be very close. There are some fundamental differences between Operating Profit and Net Profit, which we are skipping here but recommend you discuss with your most important relationship – your accountant.

Again though, in a start-up that isn't capital intensive, Operating Profit and Net Profit can be exactly the same number.

But that's not the number that shows up in your bank account!

5) Balance Sheet Items

Alongside your P&L Statement, you need to be reviewing your Balance Sheet regularly. Yet this formal accounting document is usually poorly understood and unappreciated.

If your cash position doesn't reflect your Operating Profit, it's probably because of changes in your Balance Sheet. Some of the most common culprits:

Inventory: Do you buy or manufacture stock before your sell it? Does it sit in your warehouse (or garage) for a while before it can be sold and shipped? This will impact your Cash Flow!

Why? Because you pay for it this month (cash out the door) but you don't receive revenue (cash in the door) for selling it until next month, or even later. While it's sitting there, that Inventory is an Asset in your business – so it's supposed to be recorded on your Balance Sheet.

This can act in reverse as well, if you suddenly sell a lot of stockpiled inventory without replacing it. You Revenue will shoot up, but your Variable Costs will stay low (because you didn't buy any more product this month).

You'll look super profitable, and your bank account will look great ... but without that stock on hand, you might struggle to make or deliver sales next month.

Balancing how much inventory to stockpile can be complex, especially as you grow. Keep a good record of inventory movements and it will help you predict your Cash Flow.

Loans: Depending on your jurisdiction, some outgoing cash can't be treated as a 'Cost' on the P&L. If you pay cash for an expensive new car, for example – the tax regulators in your country may force you to 'Depreciate' that expense over a period of time.

For the purposes of a simple example, say it's a $50,000 truck that has to be depreciated over 5 years: this means your P&L Statement will only show a 'Cost' of $10,000 each year.

In the first year, when you've spent $50,000 in cash and only claimed $10,000 as a Cost you will have a big Cash Flow shortfall; in the subsequent years however, you can claim the $10,000 without spending any cash to the discrepancy will work in your favour.

Or say you borrow money to make a large purchase. In some regions, you can claim the Interest Payments as a Cost but not the Principal Repayments. So again, that's a real cash outlay that doesn't show up when calculating your Net Profit.

Debtors: This is an important enough topic to warrant its own Chapter in this Guide (see Chapter 30). As it related to Cash Flow, it's important to appreciate that some of your clients will pay you immediately (Cash on Delivery can be a great business model; Prepayment is even better!) but many clients, especially large companies or corporations, may not pay you for 90 days after your send them the invoice.

These late payments are Debtors, and again should be recorded on your Balance Sheet. If they increase substantially, which often happens if you're growing fast, that usually means work done and costs incurred for which no cash has been received.

Similarly, if you can take a long Debtors list and bring it under control, or treat your Creditors differently (but ethically) that usually means an influx of cash to help.

6) Tax

Tax is your government's way of congratulating you on business success. Of course, it doesn't usually feel like that! In your first year of business, you may not have many Tax obligations to worry about.

It can affect your Cash Flow eventually though, so be aware of some best practice tips:

If you have a Value Added Tax (VAT, GST, etc) in your jurisdiction, it's usually easiest to immediately take any of that Tax collected and store it in a separate bank account where you won't be tempted to spend it.

It's also ideal to set aside your projected Business Taxes, so you have them when required. In reality, this will be a large portion of your revenue so you may need (or take the risk and choose) to use that money as working capital to fund other expenses.

Tracking the Tax likely to be owed in a spreadsheet or similar can help make sure you take risks without acting risky, and a good accountant will help you schedule tax payments so you can forecast your cash flow accordingly.

Different countries have a variety of different taxes, so be aware of things like Payroll Tax, Fringe Benefits Tax, National Insurance and so on – especially those that are a percentage of revenue that kick-in once you achieve a certain level of revenue, as they can be an unpleasant surprise.

Personal Income Tax is similar, in this context, to Business Taxes. It's cash you have to spend *after* you have calculated your profit.

A common mistake in many start-up businesses is treating the business bank account like a personal bank account, then being surprised when personal expenses can't be deducted like business expenses … and you now owe tax on those payments.

All of these Taxes can affect Cash Flow because they are paid from money that isn't usually shown in your P&L Statement.

For example, some Business Taxes are paid as a percentage of your Net Profit – so even if you have a Net Profit of $100,000 and actually have $100,000 in the Bank, you might have to take $30,000 or more of that cash and pay it as tax.

Congratulations ... I guess?

One of the Steps successful business owners do in the first year? Implement solid, simple, financial reporting and get the help they need to understand their P&L and Balance Sheet every time they look at them.

By Shan Naqvi & Jacob Aldridge

Debtors (and Creditors)

Chapter 31

As we saw briefly in the previous chapter on Cash Flow, having out-of-control or growing Debtors can mean a profitable business still struggles to pay its bills, tax, and other obligations on time.

This is one of the most common exercises we run with established businesses. They feel super profitable, they ought to have lots of revenue, yet they are still struggling with Cash Flow month after month.

First, we look at Creditors. This is also known as 'Accounts Payable' – it's the people you owe money to, and your system for paying them. It can be tempting in a start-up when you have the cash to just pay every bill the day it arrives – *neither a borrower nor a lender be* as we learned from Shakespeare.

Of course, both the character who spoke those lines and the recipient (Polonius and his son Laertes in *Hamlet*) ended up dead.

Pay your Creditors on time – neither too early, nor too late. This has two benefits for your start-up business.

First, it keeps cash in your bank account for longer. Why spend $1,000 today when you can keep it for another week? Much like learning to swimming in Chapter 1, it's hard to truly explain the benefits of this extra time to someone who hasn't had Cash Flow dramas yet – you might have to take our word for it.

The second reason is easier to understand: paying your bills is a task you have to complete in your business, so paying bills twice a month rather than every day saves you a LOT of work each month. Your time is valuable.

Lastly on Creditors, it may happen that at some point you are unable to pay your bills on time. If this happens, be honest with yourself and with your Creditors – don't pretend it hasn't happened, and don't ignore their phone calls and messages.

Other business owners and accounts people understand that this can happen – what we appreciate is someone who calls us first to admit that they won't pay their bill on time.

Maybe you can negotiate a payment plan. Maybe, if things are really tough for you, you can even negotiate the amount of the invoice.

Even just saying "I will pay you next week instead, and I'm sorry" can protect your reputation and those relationships. Just don't make a habit out of late payment – I've accepted payment for just 50% of my original invoice, but you can guarantee I will never do business with that company again and I will warn my networks not to do so either. They may have saved a few thousand dollars, but at what cost.

Now to Debtors, or 'Accounts Receivable', the people who owe you money.

As you grow, your Current Debtors list (i.e., the people who owe you money but are not yet overdue on payment) will grow as well. One of my clients who had rapidly doubled in size called me in a panic one day because her Debtors were suddenly over $100,000 and had never been nearly that high.

I was worried, until a quick look revealed almost all of those were Current Debtors and the increase in size was because her company had helped a record number of people the previous month!

When your Aged Debtors (i.e., those who are overdue for payment) increases, it will have a massive impact on your Cash Flow, your Bank Account, and how you feel about your business.

A large increase here means your clients are holding on to their money longer, and that money is therefore not coming into your bank account. Revenue may be strong, expenses are under control, but you struggle to make payroll because you don't have the cash.

Right from the start of your business, you need a Debtor Management system in place. This can be as simple as:

Make sure your accounting software (e.g., Xero) is integrated with your bank account, so all your accounting reports show live data about who has and has not paid.

Set up an **automatic** reminder, so that when an invoice is overdue by just 1 day the client is automatically issued an overdue statement. This isn't a rude email, just a polite reminder.

Schedule (in your calendar) time each month (or more often if required) to phone Aged Debtors that still haven't paid. Again, the first call may be polite – did you receive the invoice, did we send it to the right address, when might we expect payment? Subsequent calls may become more pointed.

Consider outsourcing the Debtors process. This may be to a team member at first – amazingly, because they are less emotionally attached to unpaid invoices being 'my money', staff members are often more effective at these direct conversations.

Later as you grow, or if this does become a major problem, you may engage a professional Debt Collection Agency.

The best Agencies will also work with you to help prevent Aged Debtors increasing in the first place.

The most common approach is through better workflow management. Are you and your team invoicing clients in a timely manner – i.e., when they're happiest with your work?

I knew one consultant who would actually hand deliver the invoice (then send by email) at the end of every onsite client day, which was when the client was feeling most happy about their work.

Poor financial systems (usually from owners who enjoy the work more than the accounting) means businesses may be invoicing for work weeks or months after it was delivered: if you don't value your money, don't expect clients to rush in and value it for you.

Have your team (or yourself) looking at your workflow each week: what needs to be prioritised, what can be completed, and what can be invoiced? A key mantra one team we worked with developed, and a key step on your start-up journey:

Stop thinking that 'Job Delivered' = 'Job Done'.

'Job Delivered + Invoice Sent + Invoice Paid' = 'Job Done'.

Implement your Creditors and Debtors System now.

By Shan Naqvi & Jacob Aldridge

Ask: Do I Need Funding?

Chapter 32

Inexperienced founders often give away too much equity for too little in return. *Shark Tank*, *Dragons Den* and other TV programs have given people the idea that it's common to give away double digit equity to get the right person on board. Do your research on common equity splits and be very careful of how much you give away.

"I have seen the devastation caused to entire generations of families when retirement funds, houses or money set aside for education has been invested in a start-up that failed - founding a business is risky, that's fine for you to take that risk but don't put your family at risk.

If you need money, you need to raise it outside your family from people who understand the risks and if they are smart investors then they will put you through your paces, which is a form of proposition validation too!" – **Andrew Vorster**

So does your business need external funding, sometimes known as 'Seed Capital' in the early days? The critical way to answer the question is to ask what you want the money for.

Business raise funding for two reasons: To fund Working Capital (your normal operating expenses), or to build your Product (which could range from a Software company that will need time to build their program, to a construction company actually building an apartment block).

If you're going to ask for funding – whether from friends, family, and fools like many start-ups, from your bank, or from actual qualified investors – you need to be able to demonstrate why you need that money.

What is it going to be spent on, and (once spent) where is it going to take the business? Asking for a round number (like a million dollars) with only vague intention does not encourage experienced investors that you are a safe bet.

A start-up that needs cash for working capital is not impossible, but does make an investor question whether you will be profitable and self-funding by the time the pot of money runs out.

By Shan Naqvi & Jacob Aldridge

There are six Types of Business Funding, though most new business owners only think about borrowing money from a Bank or taking on external Investors as partners.

1) **Personal Funding.** Nobody believes in your business idea more than you. So why aren't you taking full responsibility for funding your start-up? This ranges from Savings to accessing Equity you may have in other assets, like your family home. Yes, that means you are literally 'betting the house' on your business idea – but if you won't, it's not a good signal to others.

2) **Better Cash Flow Forecasting.** If you're looking for funding, it usually means you're worried about running out of money (and hopefully doesn't mean you already have). Better Cash Flow forecasting for your start-up may reveal that your fears are ungrounded, or that with some different decisions your business doesn't need the injection of cash you thought.

3) **Improve your Margins and Operating Profit.** If your business can't fund itself, that may be a sign that your prices are too low and/or your costs are too high. Few businesses are in a position where

they are unable to increase prices by at least 5%, or be more ruthless with their expenses. You may very well be able to fund your growth investments internally.

4) **Access Balance Sheet Cash.** As we have discussed, many organisations struggle with Cash Flow because their funds are locked up in their Balance Sheet (e.g., Debtor Days). While this won't be the case on Day One, even during the first year you may find money that's already yours – just not accessible as cash – is the funding you require. Options like Debt Factoring and Invoice Finance (where a third party pays you today for your Debtors, minus their fee) can help – but be aware that their fee ultimately comes direct from your net profit.

5) **Debt Funding.** Often the first source of funding a business owner considers. Banks are the most likely idea, but in reality few business bankers are qualified to assess your business plan and will be unlikely to loan your business money (hence the home loan refinance from option 1 being more likely). Other parties may be willing to make you a loan, in which case you may be in a position to

choose between Debt Funding and Equity Funding. See below for the comparison.

6) **Equity Funding** happens when you exchange an injection of capital for shares in your company. It's taking on business partner/s. In this situation, you have choices like Smart Money, Dumb Money, or Active Investment. Smart Money comes with other advantages, for example a distributor or strategic partner, while Dumb Money (where Dumb means silent, hopefully not stupid) is invested on its own. Active Investment can range everything from a Board Member you speak with a few times per year, to a full-time business partner (see Chapters 24 and 25) – and when you need the money, you may not have many options in the control or contribution the investor prefers.

Debt Funding vs. Equity Funding

Debt is Cheap, Equity is Expensive. As a start-up though, it usually feels the other way around. Why incur a liability through Debt that you have to repay, when you can just handover some Equity which may be worth something one day ... but not much today.

This is another Risk v Reward debate you need to have a business owner. Any Debt Funding would likely incur personal liability, even if you are structured as a Limited Liability Company, so even if the business fails you will have to repay those loans.

In a worst-case scenario with Equity, the value of the company falls to zero and the equity partner loses their money too.

In the best-case scenario though, you scale quickly and profitably – only to see yourself giving ever-larger profits to that Equity Funder for years to come.

This can also create corporate governance issues later down the track – one software company we worked with took on 13 equity partners at Start Up (some for less than $10,000), but when they went for a Series A capital raise of $2.5 million having that many partners all with a say was a deterrent to future investors.

The two founders had to buy out 11 equity partners, for a lot more than was originally invested, just to keep the business growing.

By Shan Naqvi & Jacob Aldridge

Many founders prefer the idea of owning and controlling everything by themselves. That has its advantages, but it can limit your growth potential. As I am fond of saying, I'd rather own 5% of Amazon than 100% of my own consulting business.

So do you need funding? How much money do you truly need, and for what specific purpose? Why aren't you able to fund this yourself, either personally or through different business cash flow management? Which would you prefer to raise: Debt or Equity?

Pivots

Chapter 33

No battle plan survives contact with the field, and the same is true of Business Plans (part of why we insist you spend minimal time on a formal business plan outside of requiring one for Funding).

Hopefully, you followed our steps in Chapters 6 – 8 about defining your Target Market and Validating your Idea *prior* to launch. This was designed to prevent you from building 'a solution in search of a problem'.

But even with that helpful experience, it's highly unlikely that the initial product, pricing, and market that you launched will be perfect for the long term.

Maybe you'll just need to tweak some things. Maybe Google or Facebook will launch into your marketplace just weeks after you do, sending your whole business model down the toilet.

Most likely, it will be somewhere in between – initial excitement from your target market (and some customers) that just fails to rapidly build consistency or momentum.

You need to Pivot. A pivot is a change in direction, maybe small or large, that takes the aspects of your current business that are working and redeploys them in a different way to face a new solution or market.

Your Pivot may relate to your product or service. Maybe you aimed to have all the bells and whistles, and now you know the customers only want a small subsection – so find your product confusing? Or perhaps you're missing a feature that the customers want – you need to bundle more together to provide real value, or just deliver the outcome faster or differently.

It could also be the Market that you're not quite fitting. Your retro safety harness was a big hit among the 100-year-old, one-armed window washer society, but it turns out that just too small a market to build a business. Or you went too broad, and need to focus your solution and your messaging.

Perhaps it's just your Marketing message that isn't working. If you're not cutting through, review your Brand Promise and Brand Archetype (Chapter 10), then explore the data from your Bullseye Marketing Strategy (Chapter 39). Start trialling new messaging, new ways of explaining your product and your value, and see what sticks better.

Lastly, it could be that you need to Pivot your Price, or even your whole 'Volume x Profit' business model. Often, that means you need to be cheaper – see Chapter 45 for some ideas about how you could use a lower price in Start Up to create more market awareness so you can raise your prices later. It's also possible that you're just too cheap.

One human cognitive bias is that we tend to perceive more expensive things as better – this largely explains the wine industry for common people. There are a number of business examples, like Chivas Regal scotch, where pivoting to higher prices also led to higher volumes of sales.

People are strange and unpredictable. Keep talking to customers and prospects, especially those who don't engage or ultimately don't buy from you. Keep using the 'Help' cue – "I greatly appreciate you taking the time to consider our services.

As a small business owner, I would greatly appreciate your help. Have you got 5 minutes to tell me how you found us, what you liked, and what ultimately led to you making a different decision?"

Sometimes that market feedback is brutal. Not because people are rude, just because they're talking smack about your beautiful baby. You need to hear it though, so that beautiful baby can pivot and grow into a mature and self-responsible adult.

How will you continue the customer conversations, to ensure you Pivot if and when necessary (and in the right direction)?

Team

Chapter 34

Now that you have an idea of where you need to invest your time, and what tasks you might employ someone else to achieve *(Chapter 16) but* before your employ your first team member *(Chapter 35)* we want to briefly walk through how to establish your operations in a way that empowers your team to step up and deliver.

As an entrepreneurial business owner, you know that to grow your business you need to grow your team. Only when they are empowered to step up and take over will you be free to step up and take your business (and your life) to where you want it to be. So how do you do that?

Most new business owners immediately think of money: how do I pay great salaries (hard in the tight cash flow of Start Up) or use bonuses to reward and therefore motivate my staff?

You may also be aware that research has shown 'more money' is not a personal motivator. So how do we reconcile those impulses? Firstly, it's important to note that the only people who say "money doesn't matter" are people who already have money!

More detailed research has shown that money is a great motivator for employee behaviours, up to a salary approximating the average salary in a geographic area. In other words, a $5,000 pay rise or bonus won't be especially motivating to someone earning $120,000 per year, but would be highly motivating to someone earning $40,000 per year.

Beyond money, however, there are some clear drivers of human behaviour. So once you're paying roughly fair-market salaries, how do you make sure you continue to motivate your team?

Dan Pink, author of *Drive*, provides an excellent overview of what really – well – drives us all. Although he falls into some of the money trap we mention above, his triumvirate of motivators are Autonomy, Mastery, and Purpose.

But how do you take that concept, and turn it to practical steps in your business? Doing so requires an understanding of the conflicting, competing desires that motivate or dishearten us as human beings.

We each have 6 conflicting desires, some of which were introduced when talking about Brand Archetypes in Chapter 10. The challenge in managing people isn't understanding this simple list; the challenge is that those 6 desires compete with each other, and that your employees can change over time.

Autonomy is about having genuine responsibility for creating change. This is established through the competing desires of **Belonging** and **Individuality**.

Belonging in an organisation is linked to your Cultural Vision. Specifically, what Behaviours do you as a group encourage or and which do you not tolerate? These behaviours, more so than esoteric tools like Core Values, determine a culture on a daily basis and therefore help individuals feel like they belong.

Individuality requires us to remember each team member is unique, not just part of our conglomerate. This is certainly easier in the beginning, when your team is small.

As you grow, and especially if you establish layers of management, make it a key part of your leadership culture that all Directors and Managers demonstrate they know the personal triggers (things like family, holidays, hobbies) for each team member.

Mastery is about developing skills to a desired level of competence. The competing challenge here is the balance between **Stability** and **Risk.**

Stability is developing your existing skills further, and having the opportunity to practice them. You've probably worked with people who have comfortably plateaued in their career, staying in a single job and organisation for years (and being happy with that).

This is a great example of people who value Stability above Risk. As a company, you can support everyone's desired level of Stability by having clear roles and responsibilities. These position descriptions and documented workflows ensures the right person is reliably doing the right job at the right time.

Risk taking is a natural human desire, even among employees who are less risk tolerant than entrepreneurs. People still want to learn new things, to try out a new skill and learn through their own mistakes. If we deny this desire, some of our best team members will leave for other companies and new challenges.

Support your team through a documented training program with individual input, and Managers who encourage growth and support failures.

Purpose is that intuitive sense in a team member that this is more than a job that they are contributing to the world. Every organisation achieves this by adding value in its own way, so you don't have to be a charity to have an altruistic purpose. The conflict is purpose as it relates to the **Present** and the **Future**.

Present motivation ensures an individual's contributions are clearly connected to the broader Vision and Purpose of your company, and that this is connected to the personal 'Why' of the individual.

You can achieve these connections by acknowledging success, like completing a project, and by doing so publicly so the individual feels recognised.

Future purpose is more than just the longer-term vision of your company. To truly motivate individuals, they need to know that this role today is part of building their future careers.

As a great leader, you need to do this with abundance – helping build their future, even if it means them leaving your company at some point. As Richard Branson once said: "Train your team so they could work anywhere, then build a Culture so they wouldn't want to work anywhere else."

Empowered individuals and a more successful business awaits when you understand those 6 Drivers and build a business that supports them. Remember too, that your team will change over time. What worked to motivate them last year may not work in the future.

Your challenge as a leader and manager is to continue to manage your relationship so it evolves with the life of your team.

Before you hire your first team member, take the steps to:

- Define the behaviours of your Culture.
- Learn and recognise their personal triggers.
- Have documented position descriptions and clear workflows
- Offer a personalised training program.
- Acknowledge public success, in real time, and

- Take pride in building a future for all of your team members, even when it may not be forever aligned with your company's growth.

By Shan Naqvi & Jacob Aldridge

Hiring Your First Team Member

Chapter 35

Some start-ups begin with a ready-made team. Funded start-ups will usually have multiple partners already, and then a clear war chest and business plan for recruiting their first hires.

For the vast majority of start-ups, however, the question of when to hire your first team member is one filled with anxiety and uncertainty.

In fact, half of all registered businesses never reach the stage where they hire somebody. Their commercial vision (often no desire for Saleable Business Equity) and/or personal fears keep the business as single person.

That's an OK choice to make consciously – but there's a reason *Robert Kiyosaki* separates out the self-employed sole trader from the business owner entrepreneur.

The latter is more challenging, requires more risks, but truly builds something scalable and sustainable.

So what do you need to think through before you take that plunge and hire your first team member?

Unsurprisingly, there's no single, right answer: How quickly you hire your first staff member depends on how confident you are about your forward revenue, and how scared or relaxed you want to feel on your business growth journey.

Ultimately, if you're considering it, it's probably time to take the plunge. You were crazy to start your own business in the first place - and it's that risk taking approach that will determine the ultimate success of your enterprise. Taking a calculated risk about when to hire your first staff member is just the next jump you need to make.

How did most successful business owners make the decision? In reality, they decided they had to hire their first team member ... when they had to hire their first team member. They made that decision only when it became clear that no other decision (including staying solo) was possible.

It was the same intuitive drive that launched the business in the first place.

If you're not ready for it, here are some of the considerations that may help (or may help you justify it to a life or business partner).

First, you could calculate your Business Capacity (see the next chapter) now and once the employee is on board. Almost always, your capacity to generate revenue will rise well in excess of your increased cost base – either because the person you hire can do client work themselves, or because they release you to do more client work yourself.

Of course, you have to be able to fill the bigger capacity engine once you have recruited.

Who you hire is an important consideration. This is usually a choice between hiring another experienced professional in your industry versus hiring an apprentice or a less experienced person that you need to train.

The challenge with recruiting apprentices, something I see with a lot of trade based businesses, is that the plumber or carpenter is super busy with work, so they hire a cheap apprentice to release the workload ... only to find that they've got to keep doing most of the work themselves all while monitoring and managing the apprentice who needs training.

Worse still, when the apprentice becomes experienced enough to be left alone, they often use that experience to go out on their own and leave you by yourself again!

Junior staff are cheap, but you might actually achieve a better return by hiring a more experienced person who can go out there and deliver work from day one or day two. That will grow you into a much bigger business engine, and also help you keep the new, bigger engine powered up.

You may discover, by the way, in calculating the benefits of hiring a new team member, experienced or not, that going from one person to two people isn't sufficient for giving you an increased profit.

It's not uncommon to see business owners who were making more money on their own than they do at two or three people. You may need to go from one person to four really quickly to make it worth your while.

So how do you know when you're ready to make that jump? For some business owners their vision really compels them to build the team quickly. They're fairly confident with their capability that marketing and sales activity will increase revenue accordingly.

By Shan Naqvi & Jacob Aldridge

Others want to save, run hard and profit nicely, maybe even choosing not to hire until they have six months of cash accessible to cover all the bills (including more payroll) should the new recruit be a distraction.

That's too conservative for mine, it's not taking some of the risks you need to as a business owner, but it's what makes you feel comfortable to make that decision.

The final element of recruiting that new team member to your business is thinking beyond just that recruitment. At the moment when you're busy you're also efficient yourself. All you can see is how recruiting that person is going to relieve some of the capacity and to help grow the business.

You also need to be thinking that next step ahead: once they're on board, what do I need to do to make them as efficient as possible as quickly as possible?

The two most common things I see as that decision: *training* that new person, either in expertise in your industry or just the systems and processes for your business so they don't need to keep interrupting you. And then *your business development and workflow* processes, how well you can fill that new recruit up and keep them busy.

Recruiting when you don't have the cash flow

So what do you do if you are convinced that you need to hire the first team member (or, any next team member for that matter) but you are worried about the cash flow you have to be able to fund that growth?

You're balancing the growth opportunity and desire with the stress and the fear of hiring somebody only to run out of money and possibly have to lay them off in the near future. How do you get clear and confident enough to make that courageous decision?

1) **What is the actual cost of hiring this person?** A lot of business owners think in terms of annual salary, whereas thinking about the amount you would be paying per month is more palatable and bite-sized. Finding $60,000 might scare you, but finding $5,000 feels achievable.

2) **How clear are you about the value of the role?** Hiring new people generally means more revenue: will this role help you create more revenue now /

soon? If not, they may give your more time or a better life – is that worth it?

3) **Do some forward Cash Flow planning?** Map out the money going out and coming in over the next 2-3 months (you can even download a template for this from our website). Combine this with your current cash reserves (and other sources of funding, like an overdraft). You may learn with the hard data that it's not going to be as calamitous as you fear.

4) **No Decision is Still a Decision!** If you've crunched the numbers and still don't feel that you're quite ready, then flip the question: what is the cost of not growing, the cost of not recruiting that team member? Sometimes the opportunity cost that you're letting go through indecision is far more expensive than the actual cost and risk of hiring that person.

5) **Do you actually want to have a team?** Still not convinced? Then my question is do you actually want to recruit another person? If the uncertainty of the decision is causing you stress, maybe you're just caught up in other people's expectations that

you have to keep growing, that being super busy means you must recruit ... even though when you look at your vision you don't really want to.

You don't have to recruit to be successful! Yes, making the conscious choice not to hire will have consequences, but it may be the right decision for you (and it avoids the consequences of recruitment – every business decision has consequences).

In the next Chapter, we will explore Growth in your business. And you may be surprised to learn that there are 6 Ways to Grow Your Business, and Recruitment is only one of them. Perhaps the other five are better for you? Ask yourself: does my commercial vision require a team?

If so, when is the right time to recruit that first person? If you're unsure, run those tests to see if the time is right.

By Shan Naqvi & Jacob Aldridge

Growth / Capacity

Chapter 36

Great ideas fail in many successful businesses due to a lack of a growth plan – and this can mean growing too fast just as much as it means not growing at all. In fact, I like to point out that 'Growth' is the most dangerous word in business.

'Growth' sounds like an obvious choice that every individual in a business can make and then work to implement. Who doesn't want to grow?! But as we saw when discussing Context in Chapter 19, 'Growth' is incredibly vague and can lead to members of your team pulling in opposite directions while both honestly saying that they're working on 'Growth'.

Think about it: do you want growth in revenue or profit? Product lines or headcount? Do you want personal growth as well, or is it all about growing the share price?

It's entirely possible for two managers in your business, working on growth, to be simultaneously recruiting (grow headcount) and retrenching (grow profit) staff.

To help make your growth plan simple, it's important to understand that when talking strategically "Growth in Capacity" is the only definition you want to use.

Your Capacity Engine

Visualise your whole business. Think of your team. Maybe that's small, big, just you. What other resources are critical – technology, office and vehicles, referral partners, your marketing budget?

I'm going to abstract all those resources into this: an engine. Your business is an engine.

Your resources determine the size of your engine. And by size, I mean how much power you can generate. Let's call that power – the full amount you could generate from your current resources – 100% capacity.

In our engine we'll measure that as power; in your business, it's probably measured by the amount of revenue you generate.

Your current utilisation, the amount of power your engine is generating, measured as actual dollars being generated, can be measured as a percentage of capacity.

By Shan Naqvi & Jacob Aldridge

So big question – how well is your engine currently being utilised? As a percentage – 20% 50% 85%?

(As an aside, I find business owners normally have a gut feel about Utilisation v Waste; while staff tend to overestimate how busy they are – they think they're at breaking point long before they actually get there. Knowing your numbers as a whole business usually leads to having higher numbers at the top of the bank account, and the bottom of our profit and loss statement.)

Your journey to greater profit and improved cash flow begins by understanding the real capacity of your business, your team, to generate revenue. Not some mythical perfect world scenario, and definitely not the average of what your team might take for granted.

Knowing that one number can open your eyes to new opportunities. And it starts by calculating your capacity.
If you're at 20% of capacity, what do you need to do? Get more power from your engine. We call that the 'Be Better' options. To get more power from your existing engine – more revenue from the resources you have – there are 6 categories to review:

1. Better Analysis & Financials
2. Better Capability
3. Better Sales System
4. Better Brand & Marketing
5. Better Culture
6. Better Operations

Can you run an engine at 100% capacity – just put the foot down and belt it out forever? Not really – you'll blow the engine. It's the same with the team – maximum power output is possible for a short period; similarly idling the engine for too long is a problem. You want to be in the sweet spot.

But what happens when you are starting to get close to full capacity, and you still want more power?

You need a bigger engine! And again, we have 6 ways to grow the size of your engine.

1. More People & Resources
2. More Products
3. More Channels
4. Better Pricing & Packaging
5. Better Client Base
6. New Paradigm

And now that you have a bigger engine, what do you want to do? Get more power out of it.

In a nutshell, this is how a business grows.

You simply need to alternate between BEING BETTER – getting more power from your current engine – and BEING BIGGER – building a bigger engine.

Let's say you're a well-funded start-up in 'Be Bigger' mode – there's a nice chest of cash to invest, so you're recruiting more people, releasing the new product, maybe even achieving some initial success and increasing your prices. Then in a team meeting or on a podcast you listen to, a bright spark pitches a Culture project!

It's a great idea! After all, Culture eats Strategy for breakfast, right? And you have that spare cash so you can afford to invest.

You can see where this is going. Culture is a key way to 'Be Better' – it is not one of the 6 ways to grow the size of your engine. If you proceed with that Culture review right now, two things are likely:

1. It's going to take resources and focus away from your existing priorities, by forcing some or all of your team to look inwards (Be Better) at a time you're aiming to project outwards (Be Bigger).
2. None of these ideas will work (or at least, be executed to their full potential). Including Culture.

If you have a documented Growth Plan, you won't have this issue. When the great idea is raised, you can add it to the next phase of the plan – after all, once you've got that bigger engine you're going to need to find ways to get more power from it.

Or better yet, your team will be on board with your Plan – they'll understand the key Context that right now is 'Be Bigger' not 'Be Better'. So when that bright spark speaks up, she'll already be suggesting that this Culture project is a next or future priority.

Growth kills great ideas by grouping them all together, instead of sorting them into a capacity roadmap. One of my greatest delights in coaching a business is giving them the numbers and the energy of their growth plan, so the owner and the whole team can see a path forward that includes all their great ideas.

Do you reckon the team is more excited to help you implement that path, rather than just talking about what needs to happen right now, and vague goals like 'Growth'?

And how much more energised will you be, knowing you have that clear path documented in front of you?

Customers: Advocates or Assassins

Chapter 37

"Let's start with a known fact. Customers are the ultimate reason that we're in business. So at the end of the day, are you actually measuring *your* performance from *their* perspective? Do you actually track, from the customer's view, how well you're doing?" – **Peter Turner, Customer Frame**

Financial reporting is important, but can only tell you so much about the health of your business ... and more valuably, about the future health of your business. Knowing how your customers are benefiting from their journey with your business, and how they feel about that, ensures you remain ahead of any necessary changes.

Unfortunately, the P&L Statement just doesn't cut it here because your P&L Statement only looks backwards. Generally, businesses that do explore this kind of customer tracking, usually look first at Customer Satisfaction. The challenge here is that most measures of satisfaction are just a moment in time.

By Shan Naqvi & Jacob Aldridge

(Take an example you might be familiar with: an exit survey while on holidays. You give a 1 Star rating to the check-out desk when you're leaving the hotel, because nothing met your expectations and the service was appalling throughout your stay.

What can the hotel do to help in that situation? They asked far too late to fix the problem, and your holiday was ruined. Even with an apology, would you return?)

Great companies, like Peter Turner's Customer Frame, are shifting this conversation away from Satisfaction and towards Advocacy. Advocacy looks at the future intent of your customers: are they likely to work with you in the future? How are they describing you in the marketplace?

This starts with Satisfaction. A useful measure of Customer Satisfaction is the 'Net Promoter Score' (NPS), created by Fred Reichheld and the international consultancy Bain + Company in the 1990s. This asks your clients just one simple question: "On a Scale of 0 to 10, "How likely are you to recommend our company to a friend or colleague?"

Many companies now ask this question of clients immediately after a transaction. The 'Net' in NPS regards subtracting those who give a poor score (0-6) from those who give a high score (9-10) – many well-known organisations actually end up with a Negative NPS at the end!

You can build on this over time, by:

Asking the question at different points in the Customer Journey, not just after the transaction; and,
Asking the question of the same cohorts over time, to better track any changes in sentiment.

The premise behind the NPS question is that making a referral puts your reputation on the line, and so if you're going to recommend a company than you're also likely to stay loyal.

Every business has three types of customers, which Customer Frame call 'Assassins' (those with the 0-6 score), 'Apathetics' (7-8), and then 'Advocates' (9-10). And this means way more than a score. Your Advocates are the people that are out there actively talking about you in a positive way. It's like having an extension of your sales force, out working barbecues on weekends!

In a start-up, these Advocates are even more valuable because they spread both their recommendation and also

By Shan Naqvi & Jacob Aldridge

your Brand at a time when you may be unable to fund a wider marketing push. Do you know how many Advocates you have? Do you know who they are?

Compare this to the 'Apathetics', who are probably satisfied with what you're doing, are reasonably happy but have not yet felt compelled to shift into an advocacy space. Apathetics are one of the most dangerous groups of your business today.

The 'Assassins' are the people going out of their way to tell anyone and everyone about their experience with you, and why people shouldn't work with you. Advocates used to tell, on average, four people about their great experience with your business; Assassins will go and tell 12 people.

In the world of social media, any poor customer experience, poor service, or failed product can be spread to the world quickly, taking those numbers and amplifying them enormously.

If you have a high level of Advocates, you will probably be in business in six months' time. You have a positive future. Conversely, if you have a whole bunch of Assassins, your business needs to make some dramatic changes now. The Apathetics are the hidden danger in the middle, the silent group, the unnoticed, because they can switch in an instant. While satisfied at the moment they are surveyed, they're not strongly loyal so unless you are doing something to improve the relationship it may begin to slip.

Your Customers' Journey through your business starts well before they give you their money, and usually well before they give you their name.

The more you can talk to your existing clients and prospects about their experiences, how they discovered you and why they stay in relationship with you, the better you can tailor all of your business from marketing to sales to delivery to customer service to better suit those people that matter most: your clients.

By Shan Naqvi & Jacob Aldridge

Marketing Structure

Chapter 38

No matter what form of marketing you choose, it's so important to be mindful of staying authentic. Marketing is really about giving value to an audience. What pain points are you solving and how can you make real connections with people?

I ask myself this each time I post on social media, or guest on other podcasts or do a storybook reading. This mindset is the best strategy for growing a loyal lasting following instead of "fly-by" fans. - **Angela Marie Ferrari**

Do you want more money?

If the answer is yes - and it doesn't have to be - then your business needs to be continually improving your lead generation approach. Most small business owners we talk to do almost nothing in terms of Marketing. (Most also feel anxious about their cash flow more than 3 months into the future, and the two attributes are related.)

Now, Marketing doesn't just mean Paid Advertising, but there's usually an investment of money and time required to make it hum.

In this chapter, we explore the specific elements that help you establish a great Marketing Strategy.

Once you answer these questions for your customers and your business, you'll be much better placed to determine which ongoing activities (like Search Engine Optimisation, Facebook Ads, or producing a weekly video series standing in front of a blackboard) will connect you with more clients on a regular basis.

Marketing is one of those great expansive conversations that business owners love to have – let's make it specific and practical, from the top down.

It starts with the fundamentals we explored in Chapters 6 through 8:
    1) Who are your Ideal Clients?
    2) What is Their Pain?
    3) What is your Brand Promise to solve this pain?

By Shan Naqvi & Jacob Aldridge

Many start-up businesses go wrong because they focus only on themselves and their product, without thinking about the market that they're taking that product into you.

A Client Persona (and searching online will reveal a range of different templates and tools you can use) breaks down your target market ideal clients into several categories depending on the specific services that you want to be sell them.

Then start fleshing out those categories: what is their specific pain, how are they currently trying to solve it, what else do they have in common, maybe even give them a name.

You may, for example, find that your Target Market breaks down into several similar, yet distinct, Client Personas. Each of these may have their own pain, or their own way of describing (or searching for) that pain.
Once you're clear about your Brand Promise, you funnel that into your

4) Lead Generation Activity

Specifically, we break down your Lead Generation Activity into 'The 5 Attractants'. All opportunities you create for clients come one of these five:

More work from existing clients. Unhelpful in Start Up (when you don't have many clients), but critical and easily forgotten as you grow. Don't let chasing new clients cause you to forget about repeat or expanding opportunities.

Referrals from existing clients. See Chapter 43 for some detailed steps you can implement immediately.

Marketing & Advertising. Broadly, any promotional activity you pay for (in money or in time).

Strategic Referral Channels. Will other businesses actively promote and pre-sell your business, because it benefits them? This takes to time to build, so isn't a common approach in the first year of business (but is part of the bonus content when you register on our website).

Volume Opportunities. These are, essentially, activity you can do that puts your business in front of hundreds or thousands of potential opportunities at once.

Understanding how to prioritise your Lead Generation Activity is the purpose of our Bullseye Framework, explained in the next chapter.

Once you have leads, you need to nurture them and turn them into clients. That is, they move into:

5) **Your Sales Hourglass.**
The Sales Hourglass (See Chapter 40) is the part of the Customer Journey that begins when the prospect makes themselves known to you, and includes your conversion rates and long-term revenue opportunities as you grow the lifetime value of your clients.

All these elements of your Marketing Strategy are designed to help funnel the right people into your Hourglass ... so that you can then take them on the nurture and sales journey, to convert them into clients, and then beyond clients into referral sources, communities and bigger opportunities.

When you have really answered who your Ideal Clients are, what their Pain is, and what your Brand Promise and solution may be, then you will have the right information to make your lead generation and sales process smooth, efficient and profitable.

Bullseye Framework

Chapter 39

I must be honest – I used to fear failure. When I was a child, I was taught that failure is bad and the goal is always to succeed. This is not a healthy mindset! A university lecturer changed my thinking about this – he told me to consider everything as an experiment. I must formulate a "hypothesis" and consider what I think the outcome of my actions (my "experiment") will be.

"If the outcomes are not what I thought would happen, then I haven't failed, I have learned. I now need to take what I have learned and reconsider my hypothesis – what do I need to change to achieve the outcomes I predicted, or how has what I have learned changed my predictions of my outcomes.

"Then I must try again and again – repeatedly learning from my lessons. This is the way all great scientists work – continuous experimentation. The same applies to business and to life itself. We need to embrace failure as part of our learning – this is the way we succeed!" – **Andrew Vorster**

By Shan Naqvi & Jacob Aldridge

There's a million things you could be doing in your business. In fact, one of the challenges we often have as business owners is that we change 'could' to 'should' ... and start 'shouding' all over ourselves about all the things we feel we should be doing.

In reality, doing a small number of things and implementing them fully is the difference between business success and a very, very busy life of not really making much change in your organization.

Nowhere is that more evident than in the topic of marketing. You know that there's an awful lot of things you could be doing in a marketing space, and unless you're actually a marketer or have a marketing background, chances are you're overwhelmed trying to understand how to make the most of all of those opportunities.

The Bullseye Framework is designed to specifically help you narrow all of that down, by marking all your marketing options on three components that overlap in a Venn diagram.

Here's how you use it. Let's say you've got a list of all of those marketing ideas (maybe using the 5 Attractants we discussed in the previous chapter). You then want to assess them against these three criteria.

The first, how easy is that for your business to systemize? Every business is different. Don't compare yourself with others. Relative to self, is that marketing strategy easy for you to systemize or is it something that's going to require a lot of effort week after week, month after month, forever? Ultimately, being systemizable helps make sure that you get those benefits for the long-term.

The second, is it cost-effective? Again, this is you doing things for your business. I could send you a briefcase with a million dollars of cash in it and offer to sell it to you half that amount. Of course you would want to buy it, but do you have half a million dollars available to do so? It's a great idea, but how cost-effective is it really for your organization?

And the third one, does it move the needle? By that, we mean does this marketing strategy actually have the potential for a sizable impact on your business revenue? What moves the needle for you is going to change over time. When you're small and in Start Up, a marketing strategy that brings you 10 leads a week or a month might be a fantastic thing. As a bigger business, your marketing strategy may need to create a hundred or a thousand leads to be worthwhile.

This is a useful reminder about not 'Copying the Wrong Homework' (Chapter 4) – because what is Systemizable, Cost Effective, or Moves the Needle for another business may not be the same for you and your vision.

Take a weekly video series as an example. You see once that's fantastic, and think 'We could do that'. Well: could you do it? And would it be worth your while?

How easy is this for your business to systemize? Do you have any of the equipment, the experience, a comfortable host and loads of content? Is it cost-effective, especially if you have to buy all the equipment and invest a lot of time practicing and filming every week? Would it have an impact? Maybe, but in the short term only if you have an existing database.

Start mapping out some of your marketing ideas, and put them on the Venn diagram where they live. You might think about TV commercials. Okay, that's easy to systemize, we shoot it once and then it's done. It moves the needle, it gets in front of a whole lot of our target clients. Ah, it's expensive though, so may not actually be that cost-effective for our business.

Monthly blogging is another example. For a lot of businesses, having a regular blog and a regular newsletter that goes out will actually move the needle, is actually cost-effective, and is easy to systemize. So, a blog and a newsletter might sit right there in the sweet spot.

But if you hate writing, if none of your team are writers, it may not be easy to systemize, it sits somewhere else.

This is the exercise you have to do for your business. And the outcome that you're looking to achieve is a short list of only those items that sit right in the Bullseye, that score a big tick on all three criteria. That list of Bullseye items (usually aim for three, give or take) are the priorities for your marketing strategy over the next 90 days.

And in that 90-day plan, you're looking to start the systemization of those marketing tools so that they can continue to deliver returns after you go on to the next plan and the next strategy.

Your business will evolve and your business will grow. Efficient marketing is a key part of it. And to make sure that your marketing is efficient, just ask yourself: is this easy for us to Systemize, is it Cost-Effective, and will it Move the Needle?

How many marketing ideas have you already had for your business? Have you already wasted time and money on some that didn't work? (That's OK, it's all part of the experimenting.) If more Lead Generation is a priority for your business, then take the time to list all your ideas and then score them against the Marketing Bullseye.

Narrow down that short list of ideas that you can actually implement in the next 90 days.

Sales Hourglass

Chapter 40

When we go out and talk to business owners during Start Up and beyond, the topic of Sales is one that comes up over and over again. Sales Training continues to evolve.

You've probably heard of things like the 'Sales Pipeline' (which was never accurate, because a pipeline tends to be the same width at the beginning as it is at the end; sales does not look like that) and the 'Sales Funnel' (which tried to abstract it a little bit more, because a lot of people come in at the top and funnel their way down to the bottom).

I think the concept of a Sales Funnel is also outdated, because when you pour water into the funnel it washes out at the end. You miss the opportunity to capture those relationships and build them for the long term.

That's why we use the concept of the 'Sales Hourglass', bringing people in, taking them through a journey where they become clients, and then *also* building on the relationship for the long-term so you can increase your

By Shan Naqvi & Jacob Aldridge

revenue simply by turning the hourglass and having the sand (relationships) run through again.

As you develop your Sustainable Sales system for your start-up business, it's helpful to understand the eight stages that prospects can move through in your Hourglass.

Some people move through quickly; some won't move through at all; and not everyone has to make it all the way to the bottom. In smaller businesses you don't need this many categories in your CRM (Customer Relationship Management system), but I find that they're quite helpful to think about because many businesses overlook revenue generating opportunities just because they're using a simplified model.

Stage 1. Contacts. At the top is a majority of people that you may know. They're your contacts, they may be in a database, they may be getting an email newsletter and are sitting somewhere in your system. They're known to you and you're known to them, but you don't have much of a relationship.

Stage 2. Brand Promise. As we move down the hourglass, the relationship starts to develop. The first place contacts move is to a Brand Promise space. This means they now understand your Brand and your Brand Promise (see Chapter 10).

If they were pushed, they'd be able to explain who you are and what you do. What you're really looking for in sales, however, is to move them to the next step where they don't just think about your Brand in the abstract sense.

Stage 3. Engaged. At this stage, they're actually engaged with why they as an individual or a business would use your business. Beyond understanding your Brand Promise, they understand how your Brand Promise applies to them personally. Once they're engaged, you're in a position to sell them, to bring them on as a client or to develop that relationship.

Stage 4. Commitment Product. How then do you get an Engaged prospect Committed? Depending on the size and cost of your product, it can be challenging sometimes for a first-time prospect to make the leap and spend their money. The Commitment Product is an opportunity to create a smaller product for prospects to buy, to get them committing a little bit of money to the relationship.

That small commitment helps win them over the line a whole lot more than if you just try and push them from Engaged straight into the Client.

Stage 5. Client. Self-explanatory – the prospect has become a Client – but this is where most businesses end the relationship! They do a great job with the client, possibly for years and years and years, but that's the end of it. They then have to go back up and start trying to find more Contacts, more people to move through in order to grow their revenues.

We work with businesses on some of these "Bottom of the Hourglass Opportunities" as well.

Stage 6. Product Extension. The extension opportunity exists if you've sold a client one product, which they are satisfied or delighted with, and therefore created an opportunity to sell them a second a third or fourth product. As a start-up, you don't want to Product Extend too soon and take the focus off crafting your core product.

Don't forget that you can leverage partners, other business owners you've got a relationship with in order to deliver that Extension without you yourself having to develop everything.

Stage 7. Community. Most individuals these days are part of a community, even if it's as simple as social media. So what are you doing with your clients to get your business into their community, a community of like-minded people? They've decided that you're an awesome business to work with, so chances are there are other people in that community that will also think you're awesome to do business with! Over time, as you Scale Up, you might even seek to build your own Community.

Stage 8. Strategic Referral Channels. The last stage takes the longest time to develop. This is building referral channels, specifically Strategic Referral Channels. There are two types of referral channels in business: those who are reactive (when somebody comes to them and asks for a referral, they will give it) but what you're really looking for are proactive referral channels (the sort of people who go out of their way to talk to your target clients and refer them to you).

Most people are just focused on the reactive type; there's much more value in the proactive type, and it is well worth an investment of your time.

By Shan Naqvi & Jacob Aldridge

If you understand all of the different stages in your Hourglass, and then make a strategic decision about how you as a business will invest in developing those, you'll find a much higher conversion rate of Contacts to Clients and then much more revenue generation opportunities to help your start-up grow.

Maintaining a database of your relationships – in full-blown CRM software if you want that, or in something as simple as an Email Marketing program or a Spreadsheet – allows you to categorise prospects as they move beyond the Contact level. This is valuable for predicting future revenue, as you learn how fast and what percent of prospects move through the stages.

And in times when revenue is needed fast, it also helps you focus your limited time on those contacts who are presently in Engaged or Commitment level and therefore most likely to become Clients soon.

Sales Meeting

Chapter 41

Your 'fair share' of sales is probably around 30%. In other words, even a mediocre salesperson would be expected to win 1 out of every 3 engaged prospects they present to. What if instead of 1 in 3, you could win 2 out of every 3 sales? What impact would that have on your business?

It would either mean a lot more revenue, or a lot more time since you wouldn't have to have so many sales meetings...or both! More money and more time? This chapter sounds like the Holy Grail, so what are we discussing?

Let me introduce the Gratitude Sales Model, the framework I use to win far more than my fair share of sales.

In this Chapter I will walk through the 7 elements of my sales presentations – not so you have to do exactly the same process (this is not about scripting, or handling objections) just to reinforce that value in having a consistent approach to your sales meetings, and especially one that takes your client on the energetic journey through which they make a buying decision.

This is not a prescriptive agenda for your sales meetings. It is an energetic series of conversations you need to have, and when you have each of these your conversion rate will climb.

1) *Agenda*

You will walk into a sales meeting with your agenda, but the first thing you want to do is find out your prospect's agenda. Are they here simply to find out how they can engage? Can you jump straight to the end of the conversation and just start booking in dates, or do they have a whole range of questions?

Too many salespeople launch into their own agenda. Start your sales meetings by asking the prospect for *their* agenda – and give them the time to share all of their questions and agenda items. Let their agenda drive you to your agenda – i.e., meet their questions to win more business.

2) *Brand Promise*

Before you jump into the agenda, however, you need to confirm that your Brand Promise is clear with the prospect. Do they have a strong idea of you and the value that you bring? If they don't, especially if they're misinformed, you want to correct that now so that it informs all the detailed conversation.

This is not a chance to spend 15 minutes talking about yourself; this is your 90 second elevator pitch or a positioning statement from the Brand Promise in Chapter 10. Ask them how they heard about you, and what they know about your business and what makes you special.

Confirm exactly what it is that you do and how that brings value, to set a context for diving into the conversation.

3) *Motivation*

What you're really wanting to understand in this conversation is what's motivating the prospect. What is driving them, what is their need in this transaction? If they don't have a clear need that they are consciously aware of, it will be much harder to sell to them.

This isn't as simple as asking them. Sometimes they don't even know what they need! Often they will be wary of sharing in a sales conversation. It's also important that you learn their needs at both a Thinking and Feeling level, so prevent buyer's remorse.

This conversation can form the bulk of the time in your sales meeting, as you go to depth building the relationship and understanding the prospect.

I still see too many great business owners with a great product jumping too soon into their own solution and what they feel or think. The client needs spend more time talking about them, and you need to understand their motivation.

4) *Solution*

The clearer you understand their motivation, the less time you will need to propose your solution because you'll be able to anchor your solution to their specific motivation. We highly recommend a consistent, visual tool to explain your Solution.

Having these visuals keeps your prospect in a Feelings space, and also gives the prospect a personalised experience when you draw a process that will address their pain.

5) *Shhhhh*

Having presented your Solution ... stop talking! This is another tool that many business owners struggle with – you could talk forever on the value your product brings, but you need to give your prospect time to pause.

This can feel awkward for you, sitting and not talking. But understand your client: they need time to catch up, having shared things with you (maybe some that they haven't shared with anybody else) and had you propose a solution to them. They need time to connect those dots, so your silence gives them the respect that they are due to help connect those dots.

Once they've caught up to the conversation, then their brain and their body will start to make a decision and that decision will push them in one of two directions. They may step back with objections or concerns or other questions, which means you've missed something in an earlier conversation.

Go back, understand their motivation more by asking more questions, and then discuss your solution again ... then shut up again!

6) Next Steps

Ideally at this point, your prospect will go in their other direction. They will still break your silence with questions, but their questions are now going to be forward-looking: how much does this cost? What's the process? How quickly can we make this happen?

These allow you to get that commitment, and wherever possible get them signed-up or in the diary and sold! Once you've answered those questions, you have confirmed that they are willing to buy.

7) Calm

The last step is as simple as you closing down the meeting. Your responsibility in the final conversation is to calm the energy. No matter how excited you or the prospect may be, or confident or impassioned or emotional about the purchase that they're making, your responsibility is to calm all of that energy down so that when they walk out of that meeting they walk out feeling connected with the decision.

Don't let the prospect walk out on a high, because that means they will crash soon after you end the conversation. And if they crash, they may change their mind. So end calmly, remembering that the end of the sales process is the start of the relationship with them as a client.

Consistency in your sales meetings is critical. Listing out steps like these allows you to review and practice your process. Put this list (or yours) in your folder: read it and plan before every sales meeting, and then review afterwards to reflect on what you did well, and what you might do differently in the future.

If your conversion rates are hovering around the average 1 in 3, that's average and you ought to be motivated to do better. Document the steps to your sales process. Review them before and after every sales meeting.

And make sure you schedule as many sales opportunities as you can, to continue that practice and refinement.

By Shan Naqvi & Jacob Aldridge

Critical Numbers: Sales

Chapter 41

We know Sales is one of the Top 3 Priorities of a Start Up phase business (Chapter 5). And we know that this time can be overwhelming, so you need to focus on doing what really matters (Chapter 3). So what are the critical sales numbers that you need to monitor?

Here's the formula for more revenue:

Activity x Conversion x Value x Retention

Activity is how many opportunities you're creating, the number of sales proposals you are producing and pitching.
Conversion is what percentage of engaged prospects you convert into paying clients.
Value is the dollar value of your product, how much you charge the average client. See Pricing (Chapter 13) if you aren't charging enough.
Retention time is the longevity of your clients. Put simply, a client who pays you $100 per month for 10 years is worth a lot more than a client who pays you $1,000 once.

The Start-Up Business Guide: 50 First Steps

For most start-ups, I recommend completing the following exercise at least monthly:

ACTIVITY	# of Opportunities Created	e.g., 4	x
CONVERSION	% of Opportunities Converted to Clients	e.g., 50%	x
VALUE	$ Average Invoice Amount	e.g., $1,000	x
RETENTION	# Average Number of Invoices	e.g., 14 months	=
		TOTAL $28,000	

In the first year, you may not know your Retention figures. Don't be optimistic – the only person you're harming is yourself. This number may climb rapidly, especially if you have a recurring product.

If you find the main challenge is at the top, the number of Opportunities, you can add two more rows at the beginning that calculate where the Activity number comes from: Number of Leads Contacted x Conversion % of Leads Converted to Opportunities.

So for the above example, there may be two earlier rows that show 200 Leads came into your website, and 2% of them converted into engaged Activity.

Reviewing these key metrics helps you identify where in your Sales Hourglass revenue is leaking, and therefore which part of your Customer Journey or Sales Process needs to be improved.

I am often asked to deliver 'Sales Training' when the actual leak is marketing to create engaged opportunities. Using the example above, we could change Sales Conversion to 100% and it would double revenue; changing the Marketing Conversion rate from 2% to 5% would have a bigger impact, and still have room for further improvement.

Two Critical Numbers

If you have an online sales business, your research has probably come across these two critical numbers, but they apply to every business at every phase:

Client Acquisition Cost (CAC)
Lifetime Client Value (LTV)

In principle, if your LTV is three times or more than your CAC you have a great business. This means for every $1 you invest acquiring clients, you generate $3 or more in revenue. A great ROI!

You calculate CAC by dividing your total Marketing / Lead Generation spend by the number of Clients created. So if you spend $500 on Google Ad words last month and won 2 clients, the CAC is $250 ($500/2).

Ideally, you want to calculate CAC by Client Source. Some marketing ideas will be super profitable; others will underwhelm. Measuring your CAC by source helps you refine your Marketing Bullseye Strategy ongoing.

LTV is calculated by multiplying your Gross Profit Margin (Chapter 15) by the last two numbers in our formula, average Value and Retention.

One company we worked with was about to stop their AdWords investment, because they couldn't see the ROI – they were spending $1,000 per month and winning one client worth $350 GP per month. Their CAC was $1,000, and they thought the Client Value was $350.

It looked like a terrible return, because but they hadn't factored in Retention. Turns out, their average client stayed a client for 30 months – meaning a $1,000 CAC delivered an LTV of $10,500!

(Yes, they had cash flow concerns to worry about, and a lot that could be improved. But they almost killed off this profitable acquisition channel by not understanding their own critical sales numbers.)

If you already have clients, do you know the cost of their acquisition? Do you have an estimate of their lifetime value?

And whether you've done a hundred sales meetings or none at all, commit yourself moving forward to tracking all the numbers in this chapter.

The Start-Up Business Guide: 50 First Steps

Referrals from Client Program

Chapter 43

Experience has demonstrated that your best clients will usually come as referrals from existing clients. These referrals are warm leads, and you have been given a trusted recommendation.

As a start-up, leveraging client referrals can help you turn one client into three, five, or more and quickly – exactly what you need. So how do you encourage more of these?

Remarkably, most business owners never ask for referrals! So that's the most common mistake. Even those who do ask often make the mistake of waiting too long. Clients are most excited about you in the month or so after they make their initial purchase – this is the best time to ask for referrals, not by waiting six or twelve months.

It Starts at the Sales Meeting

Yes, your Client Referral Program starts when you first make the sale. No, we're not suggesting you ask for referrals right then.

If you review the Sales Meeting process in Chapter 41, you'll see the sixth step is 'Next Steps' – confirming the next steps in the relationship now that the prospect has decided to buy? At this step, we recommend planting the seed for future referrals.

In this step, try including something along these lines: *"I want to talk about our client referral program. Most of our best clients come from referrals from other clients who are happy with our work. At some future point when we have helped you, would it be OK for me to ask for possible referrals from you?"*

Don't let this stop the momentum of winning the sale. You'll see it's a soft question – you're not asking for a referral, you're just asking for permission to ask that in the future. Because of this, almost everyone will say 'Yes'. Fantastic!

Follow-up

Use your experience over time – you want to follow-up this previous conversation at a time when the client is still excited about working with you, before they start taking you for granted.

Take the time (however this applies in your business model) to do a client check or review. Make sure they're happy with your product or service, and that their expectations are being met. (Again, you would be amazed how many founders don't ask these questions and are then surprised when clients leave!)

If the feedback is positive, try your personal variation of the following steps:

> *"Can I ask, what is the most valuable thing you've received from working with us?"*

> *"..."*

> *"Thank you. You may recall when we first met, I asked if it would be OK – once we had helped you – to ask you for some referrals. Our best clients come as referrals from our happy clients, and as a growing business they are so valuable to us. Who else do you know that I should talk with?"*

Be Specific

In that example, we've been quite vague about the type of client you want to work with. In reality, you want to be specific about who your Ideal Clients are – this not only ensures you are referred ideal clients, it actually makes it easier for the client to think of a perfect match.

If we asked you to think of "five friends", you may have to stop and think for a moment; but if we ask you to name "any friends with red hair" then your brain will often produce a faster response.

Similarly, asking "*Who else do you know that I should talk with?*" can be too vague. Better to ask for something specific, such as "*We deliver the most value to female business owners with staff who are looking to increase revenue. Who do you know like that I should talk with?*"

How do I refer to you?

You also want to make it as simple as possible for a client to give you a referral, and for you to chase that opportunity. Sure, it would be lovely for a client to take time out of their day to call three of their relationships to recommend you, and force them to immediately call you; in reality, that additional friction usually blocks the referral from happening.

Much easier for the client to give you those three names, and permission to mention that 'Bob Smith' suggested I give you a call. This puts the responsibility in your hands, and makes it easier for everyone.

Another approach we quite like is the three-way email, where the client sends an introductory email to both you and the new prospect. Importantly, you want this communicate your Brand Promise and also to put responsibility for the follow-up action onto you, not the other person.

Ask Quarterly

If you have ongoing clients, it's important to have regular reviews with them to ensure they continue to feel valued. And each of those is an opportunity to ask the referral question.

Need More Referrals?!

The challenge with Client Referrals as a start-up ... is that you don't yet have too many clients who can give you a referral.

An additional approach you could use is to take any client (or any happy prospect, even if they haven't purchased your product at this time) and chunk up a level.

Instead of asking them for direct referrals, find out who their trusted advisors are ... then use that introduction to go and build relationships with advisors who work with *lots* of people in your target market.

For B2B business models, this might include asking for an introduction to (or for their permission for you to use their name when introducing yourself to):

Bank Manager
Lawyer
Accountant
Bookkeeper
Business Coach
Insurance Broker
Mortgage Broker
Financial Planner

It's unlikely that from one client you're going to get a perfect list of all of those different people, but if you're not sure who to go and talk to and you don't think that anybody cares about your start-up, go and have a chat to one client.

Ask them a half a dozen questions, and the next thing you know you'll have activity, your diary will be booked, and the referrals that come from that will flow.

By Shan Naqvi & Jacob Aldridge

Client Service Program

Chapter 44

Today I would like to share the Send Handwritten five step client retention system. I'd like you to note right up front that this is more an ecosystem than a linear, sequential process.

The reason for that is that human beings are at the centre of most B2B and B2C relationships. Humans make purchasing decisions emotionally and then justify rationally. They are consistently non-linear.

"To emphasize some points, I'm going to compare two similarly priced hotels that I experienced with my wife recently, Hotel 1 and Hotel 2.

"**Step 1 in the System is to empathize, to care**. This is about seeing the world from your customer's perspective. The simple requirement here is that your team and your customers know that you care. A team that believes that they are cared for is mandatory if you are to provide extraordinary customer experiences.

At Hotel 1 there was a challenge with parking, when we unexpectedly hired a car and just needed two hours parking.

We were told that short term parking was against company policy, and our request was dismissed as unimportant.

At Hotel 2, same car half a day later, on arrival they helped us unload our bags at the front of the hotel, quickly explained the parking options, and offered to extend our short term parking until we checked-in and sorted things out. Such a small difference in attitude, but a massive difference in our emotional response.

 "**Step 2 is to engage, to be real**. This is about team mindset and attitude. You, as the customer, are appreciated. This is about being real, human, and authentic.

At Hotel 2, every single employee we met smiled and acknowledged us, so much so that I asked if their guest-focused behaviour was part of their training. The senior manager smiled at my question and said no, it's just part of how we choose who we hire.

"Step 3 is to create a wow, to delight. Find ways to delight your customers, or your competition soon will. If two businesses are operationally similar on quality and price it is inevitable that the first one to create a wow, some theatre, some extraordinary 'extra' will outperform the others.

So back to Hotel 2, we felt welcomed. When we arrived in our room there was a personal handwritten note from the general manager of the hotel, just two bottles of water, and some local artisan chocolates on the table in our room. Experiencing such a simple welcome made us feel as though it was our hotel.

"Step 4 is to create experiences. And the reason for that is that human beings do not recall stuff. Soon after buying a new car, the new car smell goes away and it needs servicing, washing, and maintaining. What is recalled, what gets stored in our memories, are the experiences we have.

Your customers won't recall what you sold them or what you said. They will recall how you made them feel, the experience that you created for them. Think about how we felt entering the room at Hotel 2 with those extras?

"**Step 5 in the five step system is to be loyal.** So assuming absence of psychosis, trauma, or other extremes of the human condition, loyalty breeds loyalty. When things go wrong, and they will, close the loop. Apologize. Take responsibility and the opportunity to provide an extra wow. Blaming, shaming, or justifying destroys loyalty.

So again, back to our hotel, when we decided to stay longer at Hotel 2, we ended up with a 30% discount off the rack rate and breakfast thrown in. They recognized our loyalty. Not only that, we felt like it was really our hotel and we will now always migrate towards that brand.

"So the system is simple. Empathize, engage, delight, create experiences, and be loyal. But that's not easy. It takes emotional labour in an otherwise busy business."
– Greg Smith, SendHandwritten.com.au

By Shan Naqvi & Jacob Aldridge

Testimonials / Case Studies

Chapter 45

There's something that surprises many first time business owners: no matter how experienced you are in your field, no matter how knowledgeable your expertise, choosing your product over a well-established competitor is a risk.

Sometimes that risk can be intellectualised: you're probably a smaller business, maybe even a one-man band – what happens if you get hit by a bus?

Usually though, it's an emotional reaction from your prospect – their fear is that you don't have the established track record in business, so there's a greater chance something (however vague) may go wrong.

There are various ways to overcome this. Most notably, many new businesses aim to compete on Price. Your overheads are often lower, and frankly you're desperate for the income, so you lower your prices and allow clients to intellectualise that you're worth the risk because you're cheaper and they have less money to lose if you turn out to be a horrible mistake.

(The horrible mistake is when you decide to do work for free, or for "exposure". Neither of us are mountaineers, but we're pretty sure people die from exposure!)

Now, we're not saying **don't** reduce your prices or **never** do work for free. Ideally, you won't have to – you will have established a clear value proposition, target market, marketing database, and sales process so that potential clients feel comfortable paying you at fair market rates.

With those systems and your expertise, you may even be able to charge premium prices right from Day One.

With those first clients, and **especially** if you are reducing their prices, it's important to show them some extra love and attention **while making sure they know you're doing so.**

This is often the biggest trap of reduced prices for early clients: because you have spare capacity, you also over-deliver on the work. Faster turnaround times, extra meetings, additional services at no additional price.

You want them to love you, and to tell their friends. Problem is, what they tell their friends is "This person is super cheap and does all this extra stuff for free!" Not a great referral.

So set the expectation right from the beginning: "Because you are one of my first clients, I am grateful for your faith in my business. I'm going to over-service you to show my gratitude – provide you with response rates or extra services that would normally cost more.

I'm OK with that. **All I ask is that when you've received great value, you let me produce a Case Study and Testimonial on our work together.** Is that OK?"

So now you've set the expectation right from the sales process (or shortly thereafter). They know you're giving them extra value, and they will therefore appreciate that rather than taking it for granted. And they have agreed to be used as a Case Study in your future marketing.

Once the project is complete, or the initial value has been received, make it as easy as possible for the client to complete the Case Study.

This may look like a 30 minute meeting where you ask the following questions and record the answers (by video if they are OK with that; or just audio / text for your reference); if the client prefers (they usually won't, a meeting is quicker) send them the questions by email.

Some of these are obviously not relevant for B2C consumer products.

Your Name
Your Role
Your Company

What was the problem you were trying to solve / opportunity you were trying to grasp?
How did you find me/us?
Why did you choose to work with my business? Did you look at other options?
What would have happened if you had done nothing?
What has happened as a result of our work together?
How has that helped your business, your team, your clients, or your life?
How did you find the process of buying our product / working with us?
Would you recommend us to a friend or colleague? If so, what would you say?

Here's the secret to a great case study: make sure it makes the client look amazing. The better you can make them look, the happier they will be to share the finished product with their network ... i.e., people like them, i.e., people who would make great next clients.

Have the client approve the final written Case Study and Testimonial Quote. Then get their Logo and the text up onto your website and into your sales proposals immediately.

This written proof, that someone else took the risk and chose to work with your start-up, gives incredible confidence to future prospects who may be feeling uncertain.

Skill Development

Chapter 46

I believe we need to have our mindset aligned with our plans. If we are deficient in some skill required to get to the next level of our life, then we need more education. I realized late last year that I lack a lot of entrepreneurial education. I've owned a business for years, but I don't know what I don't know.

I started going back to a local junior college learning what I should have learned years ago. It's never too late to learn more. And, today, a lot of it is free on the Internet, and, especially on YouTube. I use YouTube a lot. – **Red O'Lauglin**

When I'm talking about skills with individuals, with leadership teams, or with entire business training programs, the starting point is to go through and objectively define and measure some of the different levels of learning.

There's a challenge as a business owner – for yourself, and then for your team – that inexperienced people often think they know more than they do, while very experienced people often downplay their knowledge with awareness of how much more they could still learn.

The objective tool we use for these 'Layers of Learning' maps any skill (such as Sales, Social Media, Business Culture, Accounting, or even Handwriting, Driving, and Golf!) against four levels.

Layer 1) Inspiration. Knowing 'Why' you want to develop a skill. Before we embark on the learning journey, we sit in a space of 'Unconscious Incompetence'. We don't know what we don't know – and that's OK. The first step then is 'Inspiration', moving into 'Conscious Incompetence' where we suddenly realise that we lack knowledge ... and we have the motivation to change that.

Layer 2) Design. Knowing 'What' to do. As we learn, through education (formal, or even things like YouTube) or just through practice, we shift into 'Conscious Competence'. At this layer of a skill, we still have to concentrate but we understand the fundamentals and can apply the skill in some way.

Layer 3) Execution. Implementing this properly. Next we move into 'Unconscious Competence', where we have mastered a skill to the level where we can execute the task without needing to be conscious and focused. A classic example is driving to work, and not being able to remember any of the journey when you arrive because you didn't need to focus on that routine task.

Layer 4) Training & Mentoring. While not necessary for every individual or every skill, in some instances we may add advisory skills to our competence in order to be able to teach others.

Every skill you have – from driving a car, to sales, to the specific product your business delivers – can be mapped against those four Layers of Learning. Skill Development in your business starts by documenting all the necessary Skills, and then mapping your expertise (or the overall team's expertise) for each of those Skills.

Create a Skills Matrix

This map is a Skills Matrix for your business:

- Create a long list of skills you want to measure and develop across the team
- We recommend some business growth, operations and admin skills (e.g., Brand, Sales, and Software)

- We recommend including some culture and life balance skills
- Whittle your long list into a manageable amount.
- Depending on importance of training in your business

    (Roughly 20, but can be up to 30)
- List those skills across the top of a page, with the 4 Layers of Learning down the page, to create a personalized skills matrix

Conduct a Training Needs Analysis

Whether the business is just you, or many employees, you can now use that skills matrix to conduct a training needs analysis.

- Give each team member a printed copy of the Training Skills Matrix you have created
- Explain to them the 4 Layers of Learning – each skill will have 4 boxes or balloons underneath to signify each Layer
- Colour each box/balloon.

    Green = I have this Skill at this Level;

    Yellow = Early Application;

    Red = No or Not Yet

- Have everyone mark their skills honestly
- There is no need to go to Level 3 or Level 4 for every skill
- Once coloured, have team members circle the 3 Skills they want to focus their training on now
- Lastly, have each team member write their name and the date on the top of the sheet, and hand them back to you

Having received everyone responses (and again, at Start Up this may just be you) review each individual's responses. Have they been honest with themselves about ability and which skills to prioritise? Adjust accordingly.

You can create an overall Skills Matrix for the business by using an average of everyone's scores. This can be a useful metric for tracking skill development over time.

Develop a Training Plan

The main focus though is on developing a Training Plan that balances each individual's needs with the overall commercial reality of the business.

Rank the different Skills in order of the most requested training, and then add in what you see as the biggest weaknesses. Create a training plan – internal, external, formal or not – for how you plan to develop these skills at these levels.

The top priorities become part of your Formal, Internal training program. This is best done as a regular training session with your team (or, where relevant, different sections of your team like Sales or Admin). Great businesses that succeed run training for every team member at least monthly, often weekly.

Skills that are important to an individual, but less valuable to the business overall, are often best delivered externally (either Formally or Informally). Consider having a training budget as part of your employment package, or offering individuals a 'matched funding' program where you will pay for half of their external training as long as they pay for half as well.

Having developed this plan, and mapped out the specific content of your Internal Training for the foreseeable future, make sure to communicate this plan with your team.

Having involved them in the Needs Analysis, and referring to that data when communicating the plan, ensures their commitment.

Once you've got the team on board for the training program you put out there, it will be so much easier to implement.

By Shan Naqvi & Jacob Aldridge

Premises

Chapter 47

Even the most digital of businesses needs a base of operations, a headquarters or primary office. Deciding which is best for your start-up can be a tricky question: too much or too fancy an office space and you could bleed money, but try to cut corners here are you could hold your business back.

Critically, don't let ego impact your decision here. I've seen hospitality businesses spend hundreds of thousands of dollars on swanky fit-outs in premium locations … only to be out of business in less than a year because their product wasn't a fit for that market.

Conversely, I've seen hot businesses wonder why they can't attract great staff, when they have the existing team squeezed into a spare bedroom at home to save rent!

Answering these critical Premises questions can help you make the right decision at the right time.

How much space do I need right now?

This is the first, but not the final question. Be honest – how much space do you need right now? All those famous 'Silicon Valley Garage' businesses started in a garage because that was all the space they needed.

A home office for one person might suffice in the early days (or forever). If you already have a team, then how much space do you really need – being mindful of the staff amenities question below?

How much space will I need soon?

'Soon' is subjective, and may be 3 months or 3 years. If you plan to grow the team, how much space will you need in the near future (whatever that means to you)? The balance here must be struck between being positive about your growth, but not unrealistically optimistic.

You don't want to be paying that Fixed Cost rent on space – whether it's a restaurant or an office – that's twice as large as you need.

By Shan Naqvi & Jacob Aldridge

What Staff Amenities do I want?

We shift from needs to wants here, because staff amenities are a critical part of the Culture you are building. Want the team to eat their lunch together? Then you need a kitchen with enough space.

Want some private meeting rooms, booths for quiet reflection, an enormous hard-copy resource library, plus a billiard table? Then factor that in ... just make sure you'll get a return (commercial or cultural) on that investment.

What's my Preferred Location?

Again, the battle of ego vs. wallet. A high street address in a great new building is wholly unnecessary for a drop shipping company you run yourself; but don't try to start your dream café two streets away from the action just because the rent is half the price.

Where do your staff live? Where do you live, and how much of a commute do you want? Where do your ideal clients live or work, and will they need to come to you? Does your physical address need to say something about your Brand?

What Lease Period do I want? Can I achieve that?

As you start answering these questions, the competing criteria start to stand out. One factor is realistically what Lease / Rental terms can you achieve for the size and standard you want in your preferred location?

As a start-up, shorter leases tend to be ideal – you're only committing for 12 months (sometimes less), so if you grow then you can move soon and if it all goes south then you're not personally liable for 5 years of lease payments.

Exceptions include well-funded hospitality businesses, where fittings and fixtures may be worth a lot more than the rent (so you don't want to unfit and unfix those in just a year's time) and consistency of location is critical to customer loyalty.

What Quality fit out do you require?

Largely, this comes down to whether clients ever visit your office or not? And somewhat to the standards that your team prefer.

One IT company we worked with faced several conflicts answering these questions. Their clients were large corporate multi-nationals – so a premium address and a nice meeting room (seldom used, but necessary) were important. But their team were programming boffins, who valued the ping-pong table and not having to wear shoes to work! The team also didn't like having to pay for parking.

Ultimately, the owner found a new multi-story office park on the city fringe. It was close enough for the clients to visit when they did, but out of town far enough that parking was abundant. And he was able to negotiate a fit-out that clearly separated the client meeting areas from where the magic (and ping-pong) happened.

Having found all of that, he was quite happy to sign a 5 year lease on a space that was larger than he needed now, but affordable and balanced should he add several more team members in that time.

Worst case if I don't move? If I do?

The final question to ask yourself is actually two questions to ponder: What is the worst that can happen if you don't take this premise? And what is the worst that can happen if you do?

Usually, the worst that can happen if you do take on a lease is the total cost falling on you, your family, and your mortgage.

The worst that can happen if you *don't* take the space might be lost clients, lost team members, or lost productivity (yours, if working from home isn't your style, or your team is in the wrong workspace).

Those can all be expensive ... if they are indeed genuine factors. Because sometimes the worst that can happen is ... you need to review your work location again in six months. That's not that big a deal.

What Premises have you chosen for your business? Are you there for the long-term, flexible, or already looking to change?

By Shan Naqvi & Jacob Aldridge

Leveraging Technology

Chapter 48

Each piece of Technology exists in your business for one of three reasons: it's either a Fix, a System, or an Asset. Too many start-ups invest in Technology Assets, when they only need a Quick Fix.

Quick Fix technology serves a purpose today: it makes your life easier, maybe it even makes your business work, but it's clunky and hacky and probably not a long-term solution. Maybe it's the cheap option like choosing free Dropbox over a paid Document Management System.

Maybe it's actually the more expensive option, like using your bank's payment provider rather than Stripe, because that's faster and easier and (here's the key) **you have more important things to do with your time.**

Make Quick Fix decisions consciously. Accept the potential consequences. And don't feel guilty about them – every business is built on some selection of Quick Fixes somewhere.

Systems are the more sustainable technology solutions in your business. These have been planned and thought through, and they help your business run more efficiently.

These are naturally less common in a start-up, where the most likely systems are those the founder has used previously or relate to the most critical functions. Like every decision, when you upgrade from a Quick Fix to a System make sure it delivers a return on your investment of your time and money.

Assets are the technology systems that you implement that genuinely add value to your business equity. This means they are usually built for purpose internally to your business.

If you *are* a technology business, then of course you are going to build some Technology Assets from Start Up (and most of the advice in this chapter won't apply). It's also possible that technology solutions you find for your business may be transferable to other businesses in your industry or facing similar challenges.

Many founders have discovered that Systems built for themselves can be spun out into a new company, sometimes even more profitably!

By Shan Naqvi & Jacob Aldridge

The temptation, especially when you have spare time, is to treat something that warrants a Quick Fix like you're developing a unicorn Asset. Don't over-invest in your technology.

Leading Edge v Bleeding Edge

The other temptation for the start-up founder, newly released to make all the decisions, is to build a company on the cutting edge of new technology.

Again, you can make the conscious decision to be a Leading Edge (even Bleeding Edge) technology company where that will add value to your product and therefore your business. However, playing with bright shiny (and unproven) objects is one way to slowly lose all your Start Up energy without replacing it with actual revenue.

For most businesses, the best technology option is to follow the leader. Let other companies test all the myriad options, and when they decide what software or systems work then you can benefit from their research.

Don't be a laggard. And don't be a tech company ... when you're not actually a tech company.

So every technology decision you make, make it clearly: Are we grabbing a Quick Fix, implementing a thought-out System, or genuinely investing in a long-term Asset for our business?

By Shan Naqvi & Jacob Aldridge

Suppliers

Chapter 49

The only thing I would add in for a "physical" product business (i.e., they will be manufacturing something) is that you have to have multiple possible raw material suppliers and understand the cost implications and impacting factors associated with each one.

"I personally know of a start-up in the UK whose entire proposition was based around physical components supplied from a single supplier in China. When the UK voted for Brexit and the value of Sterling dropped sharply, the Chinese supplier demanded upfront payment for the components, which increased substantially in GBP cost terms.

"The start-up could no longer afford to bring their physical product to market at a price point that was commercially viable and they had to declare insolvency."
– **Andrew Vorster**

While all business owners ponder their employees deeply, it's easy to ignore the similar importance Suppliers can play in your business.

Caught up in the emotion of business, it's easy for us to feel that we are an incredibly valuable (and underappreciated) organisation but our various suppliers are interchangeable commodities.

Instead, we must appreciate that everyone who supports our business – whether that's a parts manufacturer in China or the stationery store around the corner – is an integral part of our business.

Are they a Commodity or a Partner?

The provider of your paperclips plays a different role to the exclusive supplier of parts for your core product.

If you *are* a product business that is outsourcing manufacturing or component parts, you may need to invest additional time and money developing the right relationship/s and ensuring they will be sustainable.

Can they handle the volume you hope to achieve? What happens if you fall short? And importantly, do you have a 'Plan B' if the supplier you choose encounters business difficulties themselves?

By Shan Naqvi & Jacob Aldridge

In the previous chapter of this Guide, we talked about a Technology business needing to have their own tech development team; that may be unfeasible for a start-up manufacturing plant – but consider what would be required for you to own more and more of the process yourself over time.

'Commodity' suppliers are readily interchangeable, and usually your decision will depend on the lowest price or some specific aspects of their service that you value.

Most suppliers won't fit neatly at either extreme, but as a simple rule of thumb: put your Suppliers into one of these two columns based on the question *as we grow towards our Vision, will it eventually be beneficial for us to own this Supplier?*

If 'No' (the vast majority of your Suppliers) then they are towards the Commodity section. Whether it's your paperclips, or your accountant, hold them accountable to supporting your needs and never taking you for granted. Be prepared to change Suppliers at some point, if they no longer serve your needs.

If 'Yes', that doesn't necessarily mean you will want to buy that company. Maybe you will need to bring it in-house (through acquisition, or just developing those capabilities yourself); more often you will continue to invest in the relationship between your two companies to create a mutually beneficial situation for the long term.

How exclusive should I be?

Having exclusive providers has its benefits, ranging from potential discounts through to knowing the service provided will always be at the standard you expect.

For critical, yet intermittent services however, it comes with risks. Say you only have one lawyer, used infrequently: imagine how difficult it will be to find another good lawyer at short notice, should the need arise.

Having multiple providers therefore has some benefits, ensuring you have access to a variety of solutions and opinions on elements of your business that really matter. Sometimes too many options, or too many opinions, can have a detrimental effect.

Ultimately, treat your Suppliers and Creditors with respect. Trust that the reliability and support you show for their business will be reciprocated should you ever require it. And if you ever feel that your business is being held back by one of your Suppliers, ask the 'ownership' question – consider an alternative, or have the open conversation for the long-term health of both businesses.

One More Piece of Information

Chapter 50

Having started with the personal focus of the founder's mindset, and guided you through increasingly specific aspects of your first year in business, let us end this Guide back with you.

Specifically, this could be the most powerful question you ask yourself, in business or for life in general. A single, simple rule that will improve your communication, business culture, and life.

Consider this: **assume there is always one more piece of information that you don't have, which perfectly explains the other person's choice.**

Stephen Covey writes about being frustrated at the poor discipline of an inattentive father on the subway, only to learn ("one more piece of information") that the man's wife, the child's mother, had just died.

In our daily life, it's effortless (and common) to judge those we interact with – for their attire, their behaviour,

By Shan Naqvi & Jacob Aldridge

their attitude. But what if there was just "one more piece of information" that we don't have about their story.

The luggage that was lost on a flight. Cultural differences for an international expat. Sick children at home.

In these situations, our frustration impacts nobody but ourselves. We fail to understand what the other person is experiencing, the context for their actions, and we punish ourselves emotionally as a result.

One more piece of information? A different context? I guarantee it exists – and that you'll be happier even if you only assume to know what it may be.

As you start a new business and embark on the most exciting emotional roller-coaster of your life, it's natural to be caught up in your own world. Young businesses can be all consuming, the more so when they factor in partners, employees, face-to-face sales, suppliers, debtors ... essentially, other people!

Yet business cannot exist in a vacuum. It requires other people to exist. You require other people to exist. And so it's essential that you fight the self-obsessed urge of the

Start Up journey, and take a moment to ponder the world of the other.

In this way, you are better placed to understand your team or serve your clients. More importantly, when you ask the "one more piece of information" question, you will find that your life is less frustrating. And in a period that can be hugely frustrating, anything that can create less is wonderful.

Here's to your first year in business, and many years of success to follow!

Shan Naqvi and Jacob Aldridge
www.thestartupbusinessguide.com

www.ingramcontent.com/pod-product-compliance
Lightning Source LLC
Chambersburg PA
CBHW021356290426
44108CB00010B/269